Media and Environment

Media and Environment

Conflict, Politics and the News

Libby Lester

polity

First published in 2010 by Polity Press

Polity Press
65 Bridge Street
Cambridge CB2 1UR, UK

Polity Press
350 Main Street
Malden, MA 02148, USA

ISBN-13: 978-0-7456-4401-1 (hardback)
ISBN-13: 978-0-7456-4402-8 (paperback)

A catalogue record for this book is available from the British Library.

Typeset in 11 on 13 pt Sabon
by Servis Filmsetting Ltd, Stockport, Cheshire
Printed and bound by MPG Books Group, UK

The publisher has used its best endeavours to ensure that the URLs for external websites referred to in this book are correct and active at the time of going to press. However, the publisher has no responsibility for the websites and can make no guarantee that a site will remain live or that the content is or will remain appropriate.

Every effort has been made to trace all copyright holders, but if any have been inadvertently overlooked the publisher will be pleased to include any necessary credits in any subsequent reprint or edition.

For further information on Polity, visit our website: www.politybooks.com

Contents

List of Illustrations

Acknowledgements

I would like to acknowledge the support of the University of Tasmania, which provided research funding and a period of study leave for me to work on this book; and to Oxford University's Reuters Institute for the Study of Journalism for a visiting fellowship in 2009. Thank you to Institute director Dr David Levy, staff and visiting journalism fellows for providing a stimulating and welcoming environment, which enabled me to complete a draft of Chapters Three, Four and Five. Thank you also to Andrea Drugan, of Polity Press, who has provided insightful feedback and much encouragement throughout this project, and to Maria Trochatos for her invaluable help in gathering material.

I am, as always, indebted to Professor Simon Cottle, of Cardiff University, for his continuing support, which began when he agreed to supervise my PhD in 2004. I am grateful also for his permission to draw on sample material for Chapters One and Seven, collected for the research project, 'Television Journalism and Deliberative Democracy: A Comparative International Study of Communicative Architecture and Democratic Deepening', funded by the Australian Research Council (DP0449505). For this research, six representative news programs were recorded and analysed from each of six countries, and four satellite broadcasters, across a two-week period (13–26 September 2004). Thank you to Mugdha Rai for her work in sorting the sample, and preparing the quantitative data that support the analysis appearing in Chapter Seven. A fuller version of this analysis was first published in the *International*

Journal of Communications in the article, 'Visualizing Climate Change: Environmental News and Television Citizenship', jointly authored with Professor Cottle. I am grateful to Professor Cottle and the journal for permission to use this material.

Thank you to Dr Brett Hutchins, of Monash University, for the research partnership he has provided since 2002, when I left journalism to join the University of Tasmania. Parts of the data and analysis presented in the final section of Chapter Five are drawn from the article, 'Power Games: Environmental Protest, News Media and the Internet', jointly authored with Dr Hutchins and published in *Media, Culture and Society*. Thank you both to *Media, Culture and Society* and to Dr Hutchins for permission to use this material. Colleagues in the School of English, Journalism and European Languages, research students Lyn McGaurr, Damian McIver and Mitsuru Kudo, and third-year undergraduate students in 'Media and the Environment' have helped me develop ideas for the book. I am indebted in particular to Ms McGaurr for her permission to draw on our jointly authored chapter 'Complementary problems, competing risks: climate change, nuclear energy and the Australian', which informs parts of my discussion in Chapter Two and which appears in full as a chapter in the book, *Climate Change and the Media*, published by Peter Lang. I would also like to thank anonymous readers for their detailed and useful comments at various stages of this project.

Tasmania – the site of one of the world's longest running and most intense environmental conflicts – has provided me with numerous case study opportunities. The analysis of the death of El Grande in Chapter Six is based in part on the article, 'Big Tree, Small News: Media Access, Symbolic Power and Strategic Intervention', published in *Journalism: Theory, Practice and Criticism*. Small sections throughout the book also draw on *Giving Ground: Media and Environmental Conflict in Tasmania*, published by Quintus Press in 2007. For permission to use images, I am grateful to Matthew Newton (Weld Angel), The Wilderness Society (El Grande) and the *Mercury* newspaper (Sea Shepherd and Paul Watson).

Finally, thank you to Dean, Mathilde, Earl and Ada for their support and patience.

Introduction

The environment was important in the late 1980s, and the news media cared. They showed this care by increasing coverage of environmental issues in their bulletins and news pages, and establishing specific environmental rounds. I was one of many journalists around the industrialized world asked to concentrate my reporting and writing efforts on the environment. Editors at my newspaper, a broadsheet based in Melbourne, Australia, were excited by the various possibilities. What's the minister up to? The department did what? The Greens won how many seats? These were political stories, infused with a slight environmental tinge. Then there were the crisis stories; the natural ones (floods, storms, droughts, bushfires) and the unnatural ones (chemical spills, toxic explosions, factory fires). These stories were particular favourites of editors. They had conflict, human drama and, almost always, good photos. A third category often did not get the run I thought the stories deserved, but the chief of staff seemed to not mind me being out of the newsroom for a day or two with a photographer covering protests somewhere in a piece of Australian bush threatened by logging or damming.

There were two types of environmental stories, however, that the newspaper didn't like so much. The first usually involved science. These often contained complex ideas and sources who found it difficult to explain their ideas in a way that could be transferred into a feature-length story, let alone news. I learned quickly that if these stories had any chance of getting a run, they needed to include some form of conflict and a victim willing to be photographed. I simply gave up on the second type. These were the stories focused on the long term; the past and the future. Why the sudden tide of concern? How firmly was it grounded in ordinary people's lives? Would it last? Was it sustainable? The word 'sustainable' was, in fact, a particular sticking point. The release of the Brundtland Report with its call for 'sustainable development' was a seminal moment in global environmental politics, yet after an initial rush of interest, the concept of sustainability and all its possibilities lost media currency. My editors saw no value in stories that attempted to unpack long-term environmental concerns and consequences and associated public and political behaviours. One night, I complained to colleagues about my inability to get the word 'sustainable' into the news pages.

'It would be easier to get in the word, the word . . .'

'Spondulicks,' a colleague suggested.

To prove the point, over the next week 'spondulicks' appeared in many stories across various newspaper sections for which my colleagues wrote, from business – where it may have had at least some relevance – to lifestyle, to sport. 'Sustainable', meanwhile, remained absent from the newspaper. With the collapse of the Soviet Union, the first Gulf War and other crises and diversions, many other environmental issues and concerns soon joined 'sustainability' in the news wilderness. Together, they languished, largely hidden from public view, for more than a decade.

Like news, this book is not entirely committed to the environment. Its focus is not the difference between greenhouse gases CO_2 and NO_2, nor the influences of Thoreau and Muir on contemporary environmental thought. Like news, it is less concerned with the 'reality' of the environment than what people say, know and do in relation to the environment. But nor does it simply use the environment to tell a story about the media. Rather, it has the dual aims of revealing the dynamics and practices behind news media coverage of environmental issues, while also considering how public understandings, meanings, debates and even actions on the environment are shaped and influenced. Many of the professional practices, reflexive actions, institutional logics, economic decisions and political pressures that influence news coverage of the environment are found in news on a wide range of issues, from war to terrorism, sport to politics, and yet environmental news is also uniquely infused with resonances of history, culture, fear and affection, of global sensibilities and local obsessions. This book is interested in teasing out these commonalities and contradictions, and in revealing related processes and practices. It is about media *and* environment: about what news media do in and around the environment and what people do in and around news media.

Why a focus on news media? News, I will argue, is a key site for information, analysis and debate on public issues. Other spaces exist; within media in the form of websites, blogs, list-servs, television forums, radio talkback; and outside media in the form of, for example, public meetings, community forums, art exhibitions, theatrical performances. However, news privileges a form and style of information content and distribution that has ensured it remains central to contemporary society. News media, according to Manuel Castells, are the key structuring intermediary in the conduct of public affairs (2004: 375). As a producer of news, journalism is a 'principal convenor and conveyor of conflict images and information, discourses and debates' (Cottle 2006: 3), while audiences identify the habit of keeping up with the news as the 'most important element' in sustaining an overall mediated connection to the world of public issues (Couldry and Markham 2008: 12). The role of news has, of course, been neither uniform nor static; its continuing centrality has been clearly threatened by changing technologies and shifts in content, which are often, but not always, related. Equally, radio, then television, then the internet have repeatedly challenged the producers of news and their diverse audiences to rethink what is meant by news, as have changing social, economic and cultural conditions and mores. Nevertheless, news has not had to work too hard to remain relevant, and this is illustrated by the fact that in times of public crisis or drama, people turn to the news. They might tune in to a community radio news bulletin for information on local floods or bushfires, or check a news website for latest updates on a political challenge, or watch the evening television news to find out more about a slide on the stockmarket, but embedded within all these acts is a belief by ordinary people that they will be informed in some way about an issue of importance to them.

The way news achieves this public trust is not easily discernible, and certainly the trend among many commentators on the media is to focus on how news actually betrays this trust. Environmental news coverage has been especially prone to this style of analysis. Such commentary often ignores what the news media do, preferring to concentrate solely on what they fail to do. Clearly, news media do fail on a number of fronts; a comparative analysis over twenty years of the number of journalists on staff in newspapers and the amount of content they have been required to produce suggests that newspaper companies invest far fewer human resources in each story than they once did (Davies 2008: 63). There are more public relations professionals writing news-ready copy, which journalists fail to check; there are more strategically staged media events, which journalists fail to scrutinize. These are important issues to consider in any analysis of news. However, by focusing only on their failures, we risk in turn to fail to develop a more detailed understanding of what it is that news media actually do. What role do they play in public debate on the environment? What responsibilities do they carry, both those that they impose upon themselves and those imposed on them by their sources and audiences? How do they convey messages, circulate meanings, carry symbols? How do they negotiate access with sources? How do they attempt to engage audiences in environmental issues? Do journalists aim to create informed observers or empathetic audiences? These are some of the questions that this book asks of media.

Why focus also on politics and conflict? Here, embedded in these terms, is a key to understanding better how the environment is being shaped as a public issue. This book is interested in meanings, messages and debates and how they contribute to personal and political decision making and action about environmental futures, both for individual citizens and for national and international communities. This interest prohibits media-centrism as any approach that focuses solely on the media, their texts and personnel, would be poorly equipped to untangle the web that surrounds public information and debate. The public sphere is filled with contending interests and intersecting flows, and the activities of a range of actors in a number of arenas drive or restrict the movement and form of information in this complex space. To downplay the role of media in these dynamics, as so much contemporary social theory has done, is to ignore a vital site of analysis. Equally limiting, however, is to draw an artificial and unbreachable boundary around what we define as media and analyse only what falls within it. Rather, a focus on politics and conflict as well as media provides an analytical key to how knowledge finds its way into the public sphere, and the work it does once there.

Such a focus also insists upon a direct engagement with questions of power. This power is not simply defined and it operates in diverse ways and in multiple forms. It can be located symbolically, providing the power to engage, influence, intervene and affirm (Thompson 1995: 17) or to construct reality (Bourdieu 1991: 166). It can be a struggle over the right to define issues and control agendas. The media provide both an arena for contest and are also players, negotiating access, shaping meanings, circulating symbols, pushing for actions, contesting decisions. They compete, negotiate, push and resist. For those wanting access to this arena, much is at stake. Successful entry can bring with it significant rewards, most notably the chance to participate in public debate, while exclusion can mean marginalization. Accordingly, sources adapt and change, altering their practices. They strategize, and symbols and meanings become part of a tactical toolbox that can help influence public debate and often penetrate political, professional and economic barriers. News media, too, will sometimes actively work to maintain control, while sources will act to challenge media centrality. That sources increasingly do this via, for example, well resourced public relations campaigns or sophisticated forms of protest and other actions is a principal area for analysis in this book. By highlighting the changing power dynamics at the interface of news media, source strategy and environmental conflict, it will, I hope, reveal how environmental issues are being shaped and delivered for debate in the public arena.

Of course, what is done with this information once it arrives in the public arena is another issue altogether. What do people do with it? Do they talk about it? Does it make them fearful or sceptical? Does it impact on the political decisions they make? How does it connect to other aspects of their lives? Do they engage with it to such an extent that they are moved to act, and if so, how? These are questions that are only just starting to be asked in relation to environmental news and its audiences. More broadly, the connection between a willingness and capacity for people to act and contemporary media practices and forms is an increasingly important theme in media research. Environmental issues and risks have much to offer in this regard as objects of study. With their accompanying political, social and economic consequences, they are a key site for better understanding contemporary concerns with media roles, responsibilities and practices. That environmental risk is both planted firmly in the local and flows effortlessly across national and geographic boundaries also allows us to consider such questions in an increasingly globalized setting. Here, we can ask how media connect with the everyday lives of ordinary people, as well as policy and decision makers, and how this connection may possibly create a willingness and capacity to respond and act. We can ask how media contribute to notions of environmental citizenship, on both a local level and towards the development of a more pervasive – and perhaps increasingly necessary – cosmopolitan sensibility.

To avoid simplistic answers to such questions, it is important to begin with a view of media as both occupying and building spaces that are always complex, and often contingent and contested, sometimes central to social action, sometimes marginal. As Stuart Allan suggests in his conceptualization of 'news culture', by breaking down the media-society dichotomy that has infused so many studies of media, 'we may better grapple with all of the messy complexities, and troublesome contradictions, which otherwise tend to be neatly swept under the conceptual carpet' (2004: 3). Here, questions as to what it is that news media, sources and audiences actually do provide an analytical focus within a more flexible and open research frame. We can ask, for example, how

6

a news text is produced – what news media and their sources do – without presuming a level of professional, institutional or social cohesion that may not exist. Likewise, we can ask about audiences in a way that acknowledges the complexities inherent in mediated communication. This book is interested in the nuances of the relationship between media and environment, and in research that has been able to uncover them. Therefore, the seemingly simple question – what are news media, sources and audiences doing, or as Nick Couldry puts it, 'What, quite simply, are people *doing* in relation to media across a whole range of situations and contexts?' (2006: 36, original emphasis) – becomes a potentially rich site for media research, rather than a place best avoided for fear it pushes us further than evidence allows. If our aim is to understand media relationships to not only environmental news coverage but also our environmental futures, as it is here, then we ignore such questions at our peril.

Media and Environment argues that the environment is a pressing concern for contemporary political, social, cultural and – indeed – physical life, yet media roles in shaping and influencing crucial public debates and environmental decision making remain poorly understood. Environmental conflict, with its raw and often bitter struggles, provides a key site for the examination of how debate is shaped, accessed and negotiated across local, national and international boundaries. A study of media and environmental conflict also raises broader questions about our shared understandings of place and community, of local responsibility and global citizenship, and about how individuals and societies act in ways that affect how we – and others – live now and into the future.

The book is structured into seven chapters. Chapter One connects contemporary and historical media coverage of environmental issues, revealing the breadth of concerns and approaches embedded in such coverage – but also emerging similarities and patterns. It shows how deeply rooted cultural forces are at work in constructing ideas of nature and the environment more broadly, and how news coverage has been and continues to be inflected by such constructions. Once such processes are acknowledged, it becomes possible to better understand the ebbs and flows in media interest in the environment and, indeed, public interest. The chapter draws together influential media analyses of such shifts, showing the emergence of the news category 'the environment' in the 1960s. The fledgling environment movement played a seminal role in the international swell of interest in environmental issues, and a relationship began between media and movement that would impact profoundly on the practices and organizational logics of both parties, a theme returned to in later chapters.

Chapter Two more firmly and theoretically connects environment, media and political debate. Public awareness and action on environmental risks are a major concern for many influential social theorists writing in recent decades. However, explicit connections to news media within this theorizing have been rare. Ulrich Beck is an exception, acknowledging the importance of broadcast media in particular in the circulation, contestation and interpretation of knowledge about environmental risk. Nevertheless, he leaves the work of showing in any detail how the media actually do this to others. This chapter outlines a framework for considering conflict within public debate, reviewing a range of theoretical positions on the public sphere and public arenas. It then introduces Beck's 'risk society' thesis within a framework of mediated conflict, and thereby points to many of the concerns raised in later sections of the book.

Chapter Three looks more closely at news media, asking how their practices impact on the flow, form and content of environmental news. While news practice continues to be studied from a range of angles and asks diverse, probing questions, such research only rarely extends to an analysis of environmental news. However, by bringing together recent studies on news practice in general with those on environmental news in particular, this chapter is able to address key issues. News organizations' and journalists' work is such that, when confronted with an issue as contested as the environment, news media will react in ways that are complex and often contradictory. Terms such as 'balance', 'bias' and 'objectivity' are heard in debates about environmental news, most recently in relation to coverage of climate change. It is important to consider the usefulness of such research terms for analysing news coverage of such a highly contested issue, but also how such terms work within the discourses of news producers themselves. However, by also considering what news texts themselves do and the acts that lead to their production, we are better equipped to gain a greater understanding of both media work and media roles.

Chapter Four closes in on news media sources. Its focus is news access; how various views and voices appear in and on the news. Here should lie a principal anxiety for those interested in the workings of the public sphere, and from this anxiety emerge some of the most important questions for media studies. The chapter reviews research that has privileged these questions, from Stuart Hall and his colleagues' still influential primary definers model (1978) to Philip Schlesinger's 1990 call for an approach that looks beyond the media themselves, before turning to more recent examples of work that is interested in how sources achieve access, including important contributions in the environmental area from Alison Anderson, Anders Hansen and others. By focusing on the activities and textual outcomes of industry and government public relations practitioners, and the voices of scientists and ordinary people affected by environmental issues and concerns, a richer explanation is possible of what sources and journalists actually do and how their actions impact on news media coverage of environment and risk.

Chapter Five's focus is the environment movement. Here, both strategic news access and symbolic power play are exposed in order to analyse the ever evolving relationship between movement and media. Protest remains at the heart of this relationship. Protest declares public dissent, but it is an inherently risk-filled strategy for the environment movement. The chapter considers how news media have historically approached social movements and environmental protest; a symbiotic relationship often described as a dance but 'sometimes a dance of death' (Molotch 1979: 92). It argues that while the internet potentially liberates political challengers from the continual need to seek news media entry, it is also proving to be another tool for gaining access into 'old' media. As such, news media are still recognized as an important arena and player in environmental conflicts.

To this point, symbols and their importance in environmental conflict have been touched on only briefly. Chapter Six explores how symbols work within mediated environmental conflict in both quite straightforward but also highly complex ways, via an analysis of media images and the case of the death of Australia's largest tree. It then turns to celebrity. Celebrities increasingly speak and stand for threatened landscapes and lifestyles, and are often associated with and deployed by environmental organizations to widen and mobilize support, and to pressure decision makers towards what are perceived to be more environmentally palatable policies. As a strategy, however, it is as dangerous as protest and has potentially serious consequences for the future of mediated environmental debate.

As noted earlier, there is still much to know about how news engages audiences, and engages them to a degree that they will participate in finding solutions to environmental risks and degradation. Environmental citizenship relies on participation; an interest or emotional engagement with environmental concerns is not enough (Dahlgren 2009: 81). Given the unprecedented and widely acknowledged global crisis that has been presented by climate change, this becomes one of the most important research questions for media scholars today. Drawing on Beck's 'globalization of emotions' and 'cosmopolitan empathy' (2006), as well as a range of research on environmental citizenship, Chapter Seven argues that by understanding better how environmental images, words and symbols carried by the news media can connect with the everyday lives of people, we can begin to understand how ordinary people – as well as policy and decision makers – may find a willingness and capacity to respond and act. The book concludes by asking how the practices and processes of journalists, sources, news texts and audiences contribute towards environmental understandings, meanings, debates and, ultimately, futures.

A few clarifications. As noted at the start of this introduction, this book's focus is not the development of environmental thought, movements or science but how these engage in and relate to public debate in and through news media. As such, these areas are considered in only this context. I remain deliberately broad in my use of the term 'environment', as it is precisely its shifting forms and changing constructions that are key to this book's interests. As Phil Macnaghten and John Urry note of the term 'nature' – a close sibling to 'environment' – 'there is no singular nature as such, only natures. And such natures are historically, geographically and socially constituted' (1998: 15). Likewise, my use of the term 'news media' is concerned not with the 'old' or 'new' platforms on which it appears but with the practices, logics, values and actors involved in and around its production and uses. Finally, while I include examples from non-western parts of the world where possible, these are limited. Comparative analyses of environmental news coverage in developed and developing countries are beginning to emerge (see Chapman et al. 1997 for an early example), but historical studies are rare. There is little doubt, however, that with the recent trend towards comparative journalism studies, such research will become increasingly available.

By the early 1990s, the environment had fallen off media and public agendas. It returned dramatically fifteen years later, but questions are now being asked about the sustainability of the environment, and in particular climate change, as a public issue. The global crisis in the money markets continues. Today, I pick up a broadsheet newspaper expecting to find various financial stories dominating the front page to the exclusion of all other news, but there is – albeit at the bottom of page one – an article on the release of a report into the consequences of climate change on Australia, which in turn points to two full pages of analysis inside. The report's terms of reference include both economic and environmental consequences. More is going on, and more is at stake, than simply spondulicks.

1

Media and Environments

Newsreader: It's six o'clock. I'm Kirsty Young. Tony Blair is calling for urgent action to combat climate change, warning that time is running out to deal with the problem. The Prime Minister is about to deliver a major speech on global warming and its potential to spark an economic catastrophe. He says the government is facing a huge task to improve the situation. One suggestion put forward to tackle the problem is that Britain should rely more on nuclear power. We want your views on this in our Five News Club poll today. Do you want nuclear power to provide Britain's energy? To vote, phone the number there. Your call is going to cost 25 pence a minute. (Five News, Channel 5, United Kingdom, 20 September 2004)

I want to begin by focusing on two weeks of news and its environmental content. The timing – 2004 – is crucial, a period when the environment was re-emerging onto the agendas of news organizations around the industrialized world, accompanied by urgent calls for action. Hurricane Ivan – one of the biggest storms ever registered in the Caribbean and Gulf of Mexico – moved slowly but steadily towards the US gulf states during the sample period, followed closely by Hurricane Jeanne, which ravaged parts of Cuba and Haiti before also heading for the US coast. International pressures increased on Iran, North Korea and South Korea over their nuclear activities, with Iran maintaining it was developing a nuclear power program and not weapons, North Korea explaining away a massive mushroom cloud as hydroelectricity works, and rogue scientists experimenting with nuclear enrichment in

South Korea. The UK prime minister made a major policy speech, declaring that unchecked climate change had the potential to be catastrophic in both human and economic terms. Australian news covered protests over old-growth forests logging and new initiatives to save threatened species, while in Singapore bird flu led to further quarantines and communities were shown working together to fight malaria. South African television news audiences were told of the declaration of a new national park and of scientific endeavours to measure pollution levels in polar bears. Too much water was lost from dams in India; planning authorities in the UK told a woman to remove her 'straw' house; in the US questions were asked about protection for New York's water supply from terrorist attack; and international satellite services ran a story on an endangered chestnut tree outside the room in which Anne Frank had hidden from Nazi soldiers.

The issues were covered in a variety of ways: as standard news, that is, relatively short, straightforward pieces of reporting in a style easily recognized by most news audiences, and as longer, more explanatory stories, drawing on a wider range of sources and often accompanied by spectacular visuals. On television, this sometimes made for grim viewing. Palm trees bent to the ground, waves lashing concrete retaining walls, houses balanced precariously on eroded coastlines, smoke spewing into already darkened skies, families leaving threatened homes, row upon row of nuclear warheads, mothers grieving for drowned children. Other formats and locations were less emotive: studio interviews with politicians, lit cityscapes as a backdrop; in the field with scientists peering into the mouths of anaesthetized polar bears; on the street with activists; live crosses to reporters outside official functions. Globes, satellite vision, graphics and maps were deployed to provide information about the direction and speed of the hurricanes, or the possible cause of the massive North Korean blast, or the impacts of climate change on a remote Alaskan community.

I want to concentrate on only four aspects of this large and complex coverage, and thereby raise some of the principal concerns of this book. Firstly, in September 2004, climate change had not yet emerged within the media as a global environmental crisis, although evidence suggests it was well on its way with significant if not steady rises in the quantity of mainstream media coverage in both the United States and United Kingdom from 2001 onwards (see Boykoff and Boykoff 2007; Carvalho 2007). Form and content were not fixed in relation to the complicated issue. This left a great deal of room for conflict and contestation. Sources vied to have their messages heard, or to dominate debate, while professional journalistic practices ensured the issue only slowly emerged from 'contested science' to 'global crisis'. In the face of scientific, political and economic complexity, the slow speed with which certainty and consensus emerged, and the high levels of conflict, many journalists and their news organizations invoked the norm of 'balance' to tiptoe their way through the issue (Boykoff and Boykoff 2004). Scientific claims also became entangled within existing ideologies of media organizations (Carvalho 2007). My point here is that to understand media roles in the communication and acknowledgement of the environment as an issue, even a crisis, we need to look directly at news coverage, at the product, but also at the often hidden practices behind it. This means both the activities of the journalists and their sources, and the highly conflictual arena within which they operate.

Likewise, my second point reinforces the need for an approach that allows us to look around corners. The key to understanding news is found in its norms and values, in its professional and organizational practices, among political economy and institutional logics, but is also present in its endeavours to actively engage audiences, via, for example, an invitation to call into a Channel Five News poll and express an opinion on nuclear energy. When that invitation is accompanied by a story on the impacts of climate change, which includes a shot of a small red-headed girl in a blue bikini building a sandcastle on an English beach, we need to consider how such images might resonate with a UK television news audience – particularly if, in the next shot, the small sandcastle is washed away by the rising tide. Despite clear failures on the part of the news media on a number of fronts, climate change did emerge as a global crisis, and one in which was embedded a call for response and action. That this call was heeded was evidenced across much of the industrialized world – politically, through pressure for national governments to sign up to international treaties on climate change; economically, through attempts to introduce carbon trading schemes and more localized and individualized measures to reduce emissions; and socially and culturally, with the emergence of a widespread awareness of climate change as a concern and the embedding of this concern within cultural products from advertising, to lifestyle programs, to film (Lindahl Elliot 2006: 233). Thus, we need to look beyond the more discursive, word-based content of media to the symbols and images embedded within them and ask how they circulate and influence what we know and, importantly, might do about the environment.

To illustrate the third aspect, let me compare two stories, one on the impact of global warming on the Kiribas Islands and one on the impact of Hurricane Jeanne on Haiti. They are seemingly separate issues, but note the similarities in images and sequencing. Both items begin with mid shots of local residents wading slowly through water – peacefully in Kiribati, post storm in Haiti. A montage of more intimate shots follows, close-ups of faces, wading legs, followed by distant shots establishing place. The next images are domestic: damaged homes, removing debris from gardens, a cemetery washed into the sea in Kiribati, bodies in Haiti. Moving from domestic to aerial shots, both stories take viewers from an intimate vision of personal loss to the multiplication of this loss and finally the magnitude of the disasters as seen from above. They then cut to their first 'authority' interviews, politicians and aid workers. Mid shots follow, dwelling on more debris, more flooded homes. Both stories return briefly to authority interviews, before closing with another montage of images: in Kiribati, children play, residents sing hymns and pray, a man carries a fish from the ocean, the sun rises over the threatened island; in Haiti, workers transfer bags of rice into a truck, trucks move in a convoy through flood waters, a truck – leaning precariously to one side – stuck. One story finishes with hope, the other despair, but the replicated flow and relay of visuals clearly help connect the two seemingly separate crises. That one crisis is about a highly politicized topic while the other simply cries out for action makes the connection analytically more compelling. We need to be highly attuned to the complexity of such connections and intersections, both symbolic and strategic, which are formed in and around public representations, debates and resolutions on the environment, and to how such connections potentially evoke in audiences a willingness and capacity to respond. As the internet and other new digital technologies create even greater shifts in the form, production and circulation of news, this becomes a more important ambition if we recognize the role of media in communicating environmental knowledge, not only of the risks but also in revealing how audiences might, in fact, act.

For my final point, I have included the full text and summary shot list of a brief story that was run on the satellite station CNNI's *World Report*.

Presenter: A chestnut tree that was featured in the diary of a young Holocaust victim is now in danger. The tree has been growing outside the building where Anne Frank and her family hid from Nazi soldiers during World War II. Museum officials in Amsterdam say the tree was an important symbol for Anne.
[visual of tree, external of house, secret hiding place in house, diary, recreation of Frank looking out of the window]

Interviewee: Anne Frank writes in her diary a lot about what is happening inside the house, the danger they feel, but she also writes about freedom, about her love for nature, and inside the secret hiding place, you can't look outside and you couldn't be seen from the outside, except for one place. There was a small window where you could look outside where you could see what kind of weather it was and there was the chestnut tree to be seen and it symbolizes her longing for freedom. [visual of passage from diary]

Presenter voice-over: Now the 150-year-old tree has contracted a fungus that has left it hollow and in danger of collapsing but seedlings have been taken from it so that the tree can live on. (World Report, CNNI, 16 September 2004)

Nature is not always big. Every crisis, every risk, even every place, is relative. People can feel affinity with a park, a region, or the globe, and all at the same time. They can fear the loss of a species, clean drinking water or the coastline. Or they can care only for a single tree, which for them symbolizes nature and/or freedom. And, in turn, the single tree can become a symbol for others. The 'environment' that is the subject of mediated public debate is constructed through complex processes of knowledge transfer, meaning making and symbolic interplay. Cultural resonances, many rooted in history and grounded to place, help produce shared but also contested notions of 'the environment' and its value. When combined with power and strategy, core features of all public debate, 'the environment' becomes a site of contending interests and political intervention, but also a site where emotions run deep. To understand what happens in and around the media in relation to environmental debate, we need to be as aware of these emotional pulls as we are of power, strategy and professional routines and practices. As such, this chapter now turns to the processes that work to influence our understandings of the environment. The following sections will return to focus more fully on media and their historic role in constructing risk and environmental problems.

Constructing the environment

There is little agreement on when 'the environment' began. It could have been 1962 when Rachel Carson published *Silent Spring* with its compelling opening fable connecting human activity, science and nature. 'No witchcraft, no enemy action had silenced the rebirth of new life in this stricken world,' she wrote. 'The people had done it themselves' (Carson 1962: 22). Or perhaps it was 1970 and the first Earth Day (Hannigan 2006: 1), a communal display of public concern and care. More recently, commentators, including Al Gore (Guggenheim 2006), have preferred to date the onset of 'the environment' to 1968 and the publication of the image 'Earthrise', two days after Apollo 8's return to earth, which revealed for the first time the planet's fragility (see Cosgrove 1994). In the United Kingdom, 'the environment' was invented during the post-war period when public policy was directed towards rapid urban change and modernization, as well as a series of international pollution incidents in the 1960s (Lowe and Goyder 1983; Macnaghten and Urry 1998). If one lives in Australia, as I do, 'the environment' began in earnest in the late 1960s through to 1972 when Lake Pedder, and its almost kilometre-wide quartzite beach surrounded by a ring of glacial-scarred mountains, finally disappeared under water and became a hydroelectricity dam (Lohrey 2002).

For others, however, 'the environment' began in the late 1800s with John Muir, who wrote 'thousands of tired, nerve-shaken, over-civilized people are beginning to find out that going to the mountains is going home' (quoted in Nash 2001: 140), or with Thoreau, who noted in his journal in 1856 of the inseparability of humans and nature, 'It is vain to dream of wildness distant from ourselves. There is none such. It is the bog in our brain and bowels, the primitive vigour of Nature in us, that inspires that dream' (quoted in Schama 1995: 578). For some, it began with romanticism and its reactions against the science of the Enlightenment (Hay 2002: 4) or to revelations about the wonders and majesty of the universe (Nash 2001: 45), which brought with it a celebration of pre-industrial times. Before that, 'the environment' existed as the harsh and unforgiving place of the Bible, the dank and gloomy world of Beowulf, the source of frightening cries of the Ancient Greeks, the subject of Lucretius' lament that so much of the earth was 'greedily possessed by mountains and the forests of wild beasts', and where Jesus spent forty days being tempted by Satan (Torrance 1998: xx; Head 2000: 56; Nash 2001: 45).

I can do no more here than hint at the historical and cultural depth of meanings, ideas and shared understandings that have built up about nature and in so doing created its later incarnation of 'the environment'. In the symbolic flows, convergences and clashes around each of these moments in history, 'the environment' has emerged as one of the most significant issues for contemporary publics and individuals. Resonances continue to circulate that, in turn, contribute further to its construction. Of course, here the processes and practices at work are not ecological ones, but social and cultural. They require us to think about human relations and communication, about discourse and power. This does not deny the reality of nature or environmental risks, but acknowledges that social and cultural conditions are always involved in what people know and do about them, *and* in their creation as a risk to be concerned about or an environment worthy of our fear or our care. To Phil Macnaghten and John Urry, the key to understanding these processes are social practices, which 'produce, reproduce and transform different natures and different values', and which are structured by the flows 'within and across national boundaries of signs, images, information, money, people as well as noxious substances' (1998: 2):

> once we acknowledge that ideas of nature both have been, and cur-
> rently are, fundamentally intertwined with dominant ideas of society,
> we need to address what ideas of society and of ordering become
> reproduced, legitimated, excluded, validated, and so on, through
> appeals to nature or the natural. And the project of determining what
> is a natural impact becomes as much a social and cultural project as it
> is 'purely' scientific. (Macnaghten and Urry 1998: 15)

Consider 'wilderness', surely the most untouched, 'unconstructed' form of the environment, and – as a specific example of the complex and contentious processes at work – the Tasmanian Wilderness World Heritage Area. Totalling 1.38 million hectares or twenty per cent of the southern Australian island's total land mass, the area is defined by surveyed and mapped boundaries and clearly labelled as 'internationally significant' by its inclusion on the list of 500 or so places in the world with World Heritage status, carrying more World Heritage 'values' than any other listed site. It is recognized as wilderness by UNESCO and the Tasmanian and Australian governments for its 'remoteness', 'naturalness' and 'minimal human disturbance'. According to the management plan for the area (Parks and Wildlife Service 1999: 92), it meets the criteria for wilderness in that it is of sufficient size to protect its natural systems, is remote at its core from points of mechanized access, and is substantially undisturbed by colonial and/ or modern technological societies. 'Substantially undisturbed' is then qualified. 'Relatively minor' evidence of technological society is allowable, as is the effect of external influences, such as pollution and climate change. Emergency services are also allowed to impact when necessary. There is even a computerized model, the National Wilderness Inventory methodology as defined by the Australian Heritage Commission, to accurately determine where the Tasmanian wilderness sits within the 'continuum of wilderness values' (Parks and Wildlife Service 1999: 92). It should be clear to all, then, what and where is Tasmanian wilderness and what needs to be done to protect it. But it is, in fact, quite the opposite. Despite the authorities' detailed definitions and signposts, almost every aspect of 'wilderness' in Tasmania is contested: its values, its boundaries, its management. This has led to decades of bitter and unrelenting environmental conflict (Lester 2007).

Such conflicts are informed by more than disagreement over management plans. In the twentieth century, wilderness's reputation as 'wasteland' (Ramson 1990: 5) began to shift. Now, to identify just a handful of its contemporary meanings: wilderness as precious resource and middle-class concern (Hannigan 2006: 40–1), an attack on contemporary society (Schama 1995: 571), a gesture of 'planetary humility' (Nash 2001: 390), an elite tourist destination (Lester 2007: 110), supporting national identity (Wilson 1992: 235), denying history (Griffiths 1990: 93) or indigenous occupation (Head 2000: 56), deeply political, despite 'all its moral attractions as a realm free of politics' (Mayerfeld Bell 1998: 232), and, compellingly, a nostalgic landscape, as identified by Alexander Wilson:

> The last forty years have been a time of dislocation, of ruptured communities and irreversibly altered landscapes. One popular response to these changes, which have been in many cases cataclysmic, has been to retreat to an imagined place and time outside of economy and history. Some people propose the unlikely possibility of the nuclear family as a refuge from violence and other social malaise. Similarly, in the pages of outdoor magazines an 'untrammelled' wilderness beckons to us with entire panoramas of amnesia. (Wilson 1992: 205)

Just as social meanings about 'the environment' vary and shift across time, so too do our understandings of environmental 'problems' and 'issues'. We commonly disagree over whether we should react to a problem because we rarely agree on what is a problem in the first place. Moreover, even if a problem is recognized as an issue, we often fail to agree on its severity and the extent to which we should move towards a solution. We know there is no simple or clear connection between the degree of a problem with 'the environment' and its recognition as an issue. Yet, it is important to attempt to expose and map the construction processes as they ultimately determine whether or not action is taken. The following chapters examine in detail how and why some problems and issues are presented for public debate while others are left on the margins or rendered invisible, but John Hannigan's six-point summary is a useful introduction to factors that may be at work (2006: 77–8). For the successful construction of an environmental problem, Hannigan argues that, first, it must have scientific authority for and validation of its claims, and this is especially so of the newer global environmental problems. Second, at least one scientific 'popularizer' is needed, someone who can bridge the gap between esoteric research and proactive environmental claims and help repackage these claims so they appeal to editors, journalists and decision makers. Third, an environmental problem needs to receive media attention in which it is framed as novel and important. As Hannigan notes, this point is best illustrated by the problems that have not received media attention and therefore remain unrecognized as problems, such as the number of Canadian cities that lack sewage treatment facilities. Fourth, a potential problem needs to be dramatized in highly symbolic and visual terms. Ozone depletion, for example, received little attention until it was shown as a hole above the Antarctic. Fifth, a problem will be recognized more quickly if there exist visible economic incentives for taking action, such as the possibility of the loss of untapped pharmaceutical wealth along with the rainforest. Finally, an international sponsor who can ensure both legitimacy and continuity of the recognition of the problem is necessary.

Hannigan's list hints at not only the complexity of processes necessary for the recognition of an environmental problem, but the many points at which the validity of the problem or the processes involved in its construction can be contested. For example, science's role in defining natural impacts and environmental risks is often contested, as the processes at work in 'doing' science have themselves been increasingly exposed for public debate (Carvalho 2007: 224). This point was well illustrated by the 2009 'Climategate' scandal over email exchanges involving University of East Anglia scientists, in which the social and political aspects of scientific work were strategically exposed in the weeks leading up to the United Nations Copenhagen Climate Change Conference (COP15). The impact of such exposure on the construction of environmental problems and understandings of risk has been profound, and nowhere more so than in debate on climate change. Here, in just one dynamic, a multitude of factors and contingencies are at work. When brought into broader and always evolving political, social and cultural contexts, we can begin to gauge the scope of dynamics and influences shaping public debate on the environment. The next sections introduce media further into this already complicated mix, showing how news has been implicated historically in some of the processes described above.

Before television

Environmental concerns have long been a part of public life and political debate, and as such a subject for media. Although specific analyses of media roles in environmental communications and conflict prior to the birth of modern environmentalism in the 1970s are rare, there are some notable exceptions such as Mark Neuzil and William Kovarik's *Mass Media and Environmental Conflict* (1996) and Neuzil's more recent *The Environment and the Press* (2008), both of which focus on the US. It is also often possible, however, to glean details about media roles and actions from broader environmental histories. Sometimes, these roles seem clear, as in this example from 1860 in the Launceston *Examiner*, one of Australia's oldest newspapers, riling against the introduction of a parliamentary bill to protect black swans:

For our part we are unable to conceive of any argument in favour of the measure, and when the notice first appeared on the paper we thought it a brainless hoax. Of what special use are black swans to the colonists of Tasmania that the legislature should be asked to throw over them the shield of its protection? Neither the sportsman nor the epicurean would give a pin for a gross of them, and although the skin is covered with a beautiful white down it is rendered almost valueless from the difficulty of removing the overlying black feathers. (Quoted in Bonyhady 2000: 151)

Despite the *Examiner*'s powerful position within colonial Tasmanian society – and Tasmania's repeatedly proven propensity for high profile extinctions and near extinctions – the conservation bill to protect the swans passed speedily through parliament.

Meanwhile, on mainland Australia, the Victorian parliament erupted in 1889 when the *Argus* newspaper revealed details of an agreement between the government and sawmillers that would mean the destruction of giant mountain ash eucalypts in an area known as the Black Spur. It provoked parliamentary debate, a series of editorials and articles in the press, and a parliamentary inquiry. According to environmental historian and lawyer, Tim Bonyhady, the agreement was contentious on a number of grounds, including that it provided a monopoly to a single operator. However, it was the environmental impact that was most criticized. As the *Argus* wrote in November 1889:

The Black Spur forest is one of the beauty spots of the colony. Its magnificent timber, its sassafras and myrtle gullies, are only now beginning to be appreciated. Travellers who come ten thousand miles are charmed with the fairy spectacle which we have too much neglected. It would be nothing short of a crime now to hand over to the destroyer giant eucalypts and natural fern bowers, which could never be replaced. (Quoted in Bonyhady 2000: 272)

While this specific agreement did not proceed, the state's giant trees remained unprotected by the colonial government despite the *Argus*'s continued campaign, with many of the tallest trees felled and split for fence palings (Bonyhady 2000: 274).

In the rapidly industrializing nations of the nineteenth century, press deregulation, better education and urban growth were contributing to a bigger newspaper-reading public. Journalism transformed into a large-scale commercial operation, increasingly focused on extending into markets beyond its traditional elite audiences, while also adopting a set of professional values and political credentials aimed at establishing its centrality in the lives of its new and existing readers. That journalism constituted a fourth estate was one such value, which continues to inform the profession's role in political debate today, as well as its own internal discourses and practices, and thus – as we shall see in Chapter Three in relation to its 'twin' value of objectivity – is central to debates about the future of the profession in general, and how it covers the environment more specifically. As a 'fourth estate', media are expected to ensure a variety of viewpoints are heard in public and to monitor and make accountable government and industry (Allan 2004: 47–8). Importantly, as Martin Conboy notes (2004: 109), that despite lacking clear substance the concept of the fourth estate helped establish journalism as a mainstream political force at the same time as it was becoming increasingly commercial. As such, the journalism of the nineteenth century was a compelling mix of high intellect, political campaigning and popular culture, focused on its growing audience's concerns in order to deliver even more readers to its advertisers, while also keen to maintain a role as public watchdog.

The press freedoms that allowed journalism increasing independence were part of the broader dominance of laissez-faire thought at the time. Individuals had freedom of expression; industry had freedom of action (Chapman 2005: 45). Combined with the pace of change – in 1851, every second English person was an urban dweller; by 1911, four out of five lived in towns and cities (Sheail 2002: 12) – journalism became increasingly important in both identifying and seeking redress for environmental issues and concerns, but also shaping ideas of nature and the environment. That this coincided with more mobility and travel across the social groupings (Urry 2002) further cemented the role of media in providing newly desired and required knowledge about the natural world.

In his book *Mediating Nature* (2006), Nils Lindahl Elliot shows how these forces of change powerfully combined in the 1870s in the coverage of the exploits of a single man – Welsh-born explorer Henry Morton Stanley, most famous for the words, 'Dr Livingstone, I presume':

> Stanley has often been idealized as a kind of daring explorer who also wrote dispatches for newspapers. The opposite order of description almost certainly provides a more accurate sense of the history involved: Stanley was one of the first and most successful 'spin doctors' of his time, and his success owes as much to his keen sense of the emergent spaces and times of mass communication as it does to sheer determination to expose himself to, and survive in, hostile contexts; contexts, it should be reiterated, that were for the most part of his own making. (Lindahl Elliot 2006: 153)

With newspapers under increasing pressure to deliver heady narratives to their readers so as to maintain advertising revenue, the *New York Herald* responded by sending Stanley to find the 'lost' David Livingstone in the Congo. Circulation figures were in decline and the paper needed to look for new ways to generate readership. As Lindahl Elliot notes, 'An international expedition that might also satisfy the interests of a sizable readership in European capitals constituted a useful strategy, albeit one that eventually had genocidal effects' (2006: 154). While much of Africa had been colonized for centuries, central Africa was a 'blank space' in European maps, which had the 'effect of titillating the imagination of all those who dreamed that most modern dream: of being the first to explore an "unknown" region and, thereby, unknown nature of wilderness' (2006: 154). Stanley's journey to find Livingstone was narrated in newspapers as a suspense thriller, with the African environment a principal character. In his dispatches, sent by telegram and letter, Stanley called upon a series of established literary tropes to 'aestheticize, intensify and ultimately "master" the African landscape' (2006: 155), which included depopulating the landscape of humans and filling it instead with 'big game'. London's *Daily Telegraph* later joined the *Herald* in funding Stanley's explorations, and his stories continued to contribute discursively to this essentially imperialist project. However, as Lindahl Elliot stresses, it would be a mistake to see the role of the newspapers and Stanley's stories only as a 'discursive' process:

> To be sure, Stanley's exploits, produced initially in the name of sending good stories to the US and British press, were the beginning of something far worse, a form of genocidal imperialism that was made possible thanks in no small part to the fact that, even before Stanley wrote for the *Daily Telegraph*, his work was read by many in the European elites . . . Stanley's knowledge and experiences along the Congo river eventually made him a key figure in King Leopold II's plans to establish a Belgian colony in the region. Stanley is regarded for this reason as a founding figure in what became known as the 'scramble for Africa'. (Lindahl Elliot 2006: 160)

In the United States, Neuzil and Kovarik's pre-television case studies also show how this mix of the popular, the investigative and the campaigning could come together to powerful effect. Mass media played a crucial role in promoting social change, and as such disadvantaged groups dealing with environmental issues had to wait until the mainstream media 'discovered' their stories before they were able to prompt any type of change (Neuzil and Kovarik 1996: xii). The story of the Radium Girls is a powerful early example of how the media could become clearly implicated in both recognizing and thus constructing an environmental problem or risk, and seeking redress for its victims (Neuzil and Kovarik 1996: 33–52). Grace Fryer started work at a radium factory in Orange, New Jersey, in 1917 with seventy other women, painting the dials of watches, clocks and other instruments with a radium paste so that they glowed in the dark. To keep the shape of their paintbrushes, the women were told to point them with their lips. The women were not aware of any danger, although the owners of the US Radium Corporation and some scientists were becoming familiar with the terrible effects. In fact, the women were so unconcerned that they painted their teeth and finger nails with radium to surprise their boyfriends in the dark, although Fryer did think it strange that when she blew her nose, her handkerchief glowed in the dark (Neuzil and Kovarik 1996: 34). Five years later and by then working in a bank, Fryer's teeth began falling out and her jaw developed a painful abscess. Another five years on, a doctor suggested her now serious bone decay could be related to her former job, and in 1927, Fryer decided to sue US Radium, with the support of worker advocacy group, the Consumers League, and Alice Hamilton, a Harvard University authority and league board member. Four other New Jersey women suffering similar effects soon joined.

It was only once the case reached the courtroom in April 1928 that mainstream media outlets picked up the story (Neuzil and Kovarik 1996: 42). However, these stories focused on the macabre and sensationalist; on how, for example, the women could spend the quarter-of-a-million dollars compensation they were seeking with only a year to live. Despite time clearly running out for the women, the case was adjourned until September. Walter Lippmann, editor of the liberal *New York World*, which had been founded by Joseph Pulitzer, intervened at this point at the urging of his friend Alice Hamilton, and began to regularly editorialize against the court's decision and the company's delaying tactics. Scientists acting as consultants for US Radium responded by declaring that the women could survive. Lippmann persevered. 'This is a heartless proceeding,' he wrote. 'It is unmanly, unjust and cruel. This is a case which calls not for fund-spun litigation but for simple, quick, direct justice' (quoted in Neuzil and Kovarik 1996: 46). Lippmann's editorials and more general newspaper outrage contributed to the court rescheduling the trial for early June. Just days before the case was due to begin, the company settled in the women's favour – albeit for US$10,000 each plus an annual allowance, rather than $250,000.

The women died in the 1920s and 1930s. Their case highlighted the dangers of radium in society at a time when, as Neuzil and Kovarik note, the substance was seen as part of the 'arena of science and medicine and, as such, enjoyed a certain legitimacy that made it almost beyond criticism' (1996: 50). It took the involvement of Lippmann and other mainstream media outlets to penetrate this elite position and force the company to finally settle. However, media were clearly committed only in so far as the case of the Radium Girls fulfilled the journalistic requirement for a 'good' story, and Lippmann's involvement relied also in part on his pre-existing relationship with and trust of campaigner Alice Hamilton. As Neuzil and Kovarik conclude:

> The interactive nature of the process in the 1920s was evident when Walter Lippmann and Alice Hamilton used each other for their own ends. Lippmann's newspaper was considered 'liberal' and catered to a working-class audience, which would appreciate a story such as the Radium Girls; Hamilton needed Lippmann and other journalists to meet her goals, including public awareness of workers' safety issues. (Neuzil and Kovarik 1996: 51)

In these geographically disparate examples from the nineteenth and early twentieth centuries, themes relevant to contemporary media begin to emerge: the important symbolic role of the giant trees in conservation efforts in colonial Australia; the antagonism of the Tasmanian newspaper against 'anti-development' legislation to protect black swans and the limits to its political influence; the framing of natures and environments as empty and available, a challenge for Stanley, a 'solution' for Leopold; the credibility provided by mainstream media coverage and its relationship with the political elite and decision making; the expectation that victims' stories fit within the norms and practices of journalism – within the formal news-gathering site of a courtroom in the case of the Radium Girls; the public contestation over scientific roles and evidence; the importance of networks and 'reflexive' interactions between sources and journalists if challenger groups, such as Alice Hamilton's Consumers League, are to have their voices heard; questions of advocacy versus objectivity; and the power of media to set political agendas and how that power can be challenged by elites, but also by those who begin from a powerless position themselves. The examples also show the diversity of topics that would eventually come together under the environmental umbrella, but until the 1960s remained dispersed across a wide range of interests, from wildlife preservation to natural areas conservation, urban health to workers' rights. The deregulation of the press in the first half of the nineteenth century in many Western countries prompted massive change for both the producers and consumers of news, and to the news product itself. The advent of broadcast journalism, particularly television, was to do the same in the twentieth century. Meanwhile, 'the environment' emerged as an identifiable category in news media.

Discovering the environment

The *New York Times* appointed its first environment reporter in mid-1969. With this act, the elite newspaper signalled more than its commitment to environmental issues. It showed that, along with many news outlets in Western nations, it now recognized the existence of 'the environment' as a social problem and media issue. Before the late 1960s, a diverse set of issues was reported on that we would now put under the environmental umbrella, such as pollution, population, water issues, land conservation and fauna and flora preservation. But in 1969, along with a surge in the quantity given to these 'separate' issues in the news, came recognition of their interconnectedness and a corresponding use of the term 'environment', which – as Schoenfeld and his colleagues have shown – had slowly entered public discourse in the United States throughout the late 1950s and early 1960s (1979: 40–2). This surge in media interest and formation of a news category provide an important site of study for all those interested in the relationship between media and public opinion. Which came first? Did public concern follow media interest, or the other way around? We can also ask related questions about the impact of this surge and grouping on political strategy and decision making. How, for example, were the activities of those pushing for environmental change positioned to respond to this new interest from the media? The profound change that occurred among Western media in the late 1960s in terms of their relationship with the environment has proven a rich site for such questions. This section focuses on this unique period in media history. The next chapter will provide further context when it turns to various approaches that conceptualize the media as a public arena in which issues and their sponsors compete for visibility and continuing centrality in public debate.

In their useful analysis of the growth of the environment as a political issue in Britain, Brookes et al. question whether the interest in issues such as water pollution, resource conservation and air pollution was long standing, and that the only change was a growing popularization of the label 'environmental' by journalists (1976: 245). They tested this by carrying out a content analysis of London's *The Times* newspaper for the period 1953–73, coding thirteen categories of 'environmental' news, including air transport, flora and fauna, food, water pollution and planning. In terms of environmental coverage in relation to overall news space, they found that coverage declined a little between 1953 and 1965, but more than doubled in the next four years to comprise 1.6 per cent of total news space, and rose again between 1969 and 1973 to comprise 2.2 per cent of total news space. Interestingly, they also found that as the proportion of space given to each category shifted over time, so too did the number of categories overall. So, for example, in 1953, landscape stories dominated, taking 65.5 per cent of space devoted to environmental coverage, followed by the 'roads' and 'flora and fauna' categories, while in 1973, landscape was one of eight categories, taking up less than one-quarter of the overall coverage. The researchers suggest a cumulative pattern to explain the growth of the environment as a political issue, whereby 'as more individual problems emerge, it becomes easier to accept that there exists an underlying problem and not just a series of individual problems' (Brookes et al. 1976: 254). Stories prior to the late 1960s were more event-orientated and did not reference 'the environment' as an issue, while later coverage was both event-orientated *and* made the connection to the broader, if more abstract, issue, thus increasing its perceived newsworthiness and the space it was allocated. A 'certain self-generating tendency' then emerged. Brookes et al. surmise that once an abstract connection is made, 'it may be easier for certain types of environmental concern to be articulated. Projected food shortages and projected population crises may not have the immediacy of concrete news but are interesting once the environment is seen as a problem' (1976: 254).

As Brookes and colleagues note, such a content analysis cannot adequately explain the emergence of environmentalism or media roles in shaping public opinion, but its historical breadth is useful in helping to identify and quantify the emergence of environmental news and its rate of increase, as well as some of the specific features of its component parts. A wider analysis in terms of media outlets, if of a more restricted issue (water pollution problems) and time span (1960–72), was conducted by Parlour and Schatzow (1978) as part of a broader study on socio-political responses to environmental problems in Canada. Their analysis of four leading newspapers, five magazines, and TV and radio found a peak in interest in the issue in 1969, although the shift from coverage of water pollution problems as isolated and localized to a more national focus occurred gradually between 1965 and 1968, and in the following two years, it came to reflect the 'national and international dimensions of environmental problems' (1978: 10–11). In interview, media personnel presented themselves as reacting to rather than creating public concern about the environment. However, Parlour and Schatzow found 'no evidence to support the contention that the public was concerned about environmental issues before these were registered with the media' and that 'contrary to the perceptions of the media personnel of their responsive role, we believe that the media have actively created public awareness and concern for these issues' (1978: 14–15). The authors have mixed conclusions: that Canadians emerged from this period of extensive mass media coverage with a lack of knowledge and understanding, a dissonant awareness of the quality of their environment, and without having adapted their individual behaviour. However, they also argue that despite these failings, the media coverage of this period succeeded in 'legitimizing the environment as a major political issue and forcing the political system at all levels in Canada to adapt both structurally and behaviourally to concerns registered by the media' (1978: 15).

In contrast, Schoenfeld and his colleagues find in their study of the US daily press that media were, in fact, slow to adopt the environment as a news category, even though early claims makers had actively sought and pushed the terms 'environment', 'environmental' and 'environmentalist' in order to signify a more comprehensive approach to the previously separated issues (1979: 40). Drawing on Gaye Tuchman's seminal study of newsroom culture (1978), they identify a range of reasons why the press was more a 'thermometer than barometer', including seeing environmental claims makers as 'minnows' in the early 1960s, too small for the news net, which in turn reinforced readers' established tendency to see the environment in unrelated categories, 'keeping their social reality incompatible with that of environmental claims makers' (1979: 54). Finally, as a window on the world, the press had no choice but to respond once environmental issues became so compelling, appointing environmental reporters and columnists and making space for environmental sections. A broader view from the 'window' was then possible, taking in issues such as urban congestion and energy shortages, beyond the traditional 'environmental' issue of conservation (1979: 55).

Despite their mixed findings, these studies show a clear and widespread media discovery of 'the environment' in 1969 in each of their respective nations. International flows were clearly at work in the formation of 'the environment' as a social problem and media issue. Although implicated in creating these flows, media were also responding to an international network of environmental claims makers. The modern environment movement emerged across the industrialized world in the late 1960s, influencing and connecting across national boundaries to eventually become – as German sociologist Ulrich Beck describes environmental NGOs – the 'entrepreneurs of the global commonwealth' (2006: 105). However, local and national influences, even at the level of an Old World/New World divide, were central to the development of the concerns on which each nation's emerging movement were initially focused. In North America and Australasia, for example, wilderness issues were instrumental in the development of the new movement, while in Europe – where large tracts of untouched land are rare – the environment movement was more closely concerned with the anti-nuclear and peace movements (Hay 2002: 17). A common feature of all, however, was their reorientation towards the media.

In the 1960s, there was little relationship between media and movement. In their UK-based study of media and environmental politics, Philip Lowe and David Morrison describe this period as marked by a discreet environmental lobby, heavily dependent on personal influence and behind-the-scenes string pulling, as well as 'on the refined horror of educated taste to censure unsuitable development proposals' (1984: 83). In contrast, they describe most of the groups formed since the 1960s as having 'quite different attitudes towards publicity and the media'. Greenpeace was the most successful and high profile of this new generation of groups, leading the movement in its reorientation towards media. Its founding act in 1971 – chartering boats to bear witness and protest against US nuclear testing in the Aleutian Islands – resulted in major publicity and, four months later, the end of testing on the islands (DeLuca 1999: 2). Four years later, in mid-1975, six protesters in three rubber dinghies confronted Russian whalers off the coast of California, armed with one film camera, which captured the whaler firing a steel harpoon and landing less than five feet from a dinghy. Footage of the confrontation was shown on major US networks and around the world (Weyler 2004: 329). The media-movement relationship, if an uneasy one, was born.

In Australia, the contemporary movement grew out of the failed campaign to save Lake Pedder in Tasmania from being flooded to provide hydroelectricity. Like the early UK movement, the Lake Pedder campaigners had virtually no direct contact with journalists, preferring to lobby politicians or to run town hall meetings and slide shows to communicate with the public. There was no trust between media or movement (Lester 2007: 39–44). Nevertheless, in the closing months of the campaign, they comprehensively discovered each other's usefulness when a tiger moth carrying a high-profile protester disappeared in unexplained circumstances and a young activist maintained a lonely vigil at the lake as the waters slowly rose around him. Within a few years of Lake Pedder's loss, the Australian movement had reformed, taking on the lessons of Pedder but also drawing on influences from the US and Europe. When the time came in the late 1970s and early 1980s to fight plans to dam the Franklin River, also in south-west Tasmania, the movement was able to mount a sophisticated media-focused campaign, which has been described as the first environmental campaign to 'attain global stature', attracting international media, identities and organizations (Hay 1991: 64). As a consequence, the Australian federal government intervened and the dam was stopped in 1983.

These early successes clearly encouraged the contemporary movement and media to form a symbiotic relationship, which impacted on the practices, outputs and strategies of both parties. Overall, the effects on the communication of environmental information have been profound. With the conditioning to an acute degree of movement strategy towards media coverage, protest and other image events have become a principal means by which environmental issues gain prominence in news coverage. Likewise, symbols that carry deep cultural resonances become highly contested as the movement seeks to harness their power and circulate through the media. Consequently, there have also been shifts in industry and government as they struggle to contain the power of the symbols or even appropriate them towards their own pro-development causes. Science has also been increasingly forced to respond to maintain its central role in the communication of environmental knowledge, producing visuals and easily communicable concepts in order to participate in debate. These are all topics for following chapters. By the early 1970s, media attention on the environment was in decline, both in terms of space provided for coverage and the content of the coverage, which evidence suggests again splintered into a series of disparate and seemingly unconnected problem categories (Hannigan 2006: 83). Another surge in media interest was experienced in the late 1980s, and again from 2005. Various models have been put forward to explain these surges of interest and subsequent decline. By focusing on the media as an arena, the next chapter reviews these models and offers a framework to allow a more nuanced analysis of the forces shaping these 'ups and downs' in media engagement with the environment.

At the start of this chapter, I drew on a sample of international television news to highlight four broad, interconnected aspects from which to consider the relationship between media and the environment. By briefly traversing the historical path of nature and environment and the evolution of media engagement with 'the environment', I have hoped to show how those aspects are also deeply rooted in the past. The emergence of a contemporary movement acutely conditioned towards gaining media coverage highlights the salience of the first point; that we need to look deeply at news media coverage, directly but also behind the texts to the activities of the journalists and sources, and to the specifics of the space within which it is created and circulated. The potency of particular symbols and their ability to resonate in moments and places reinforces the second point; that we need to look beyond media's more discursive, word-based content, asking how symbols and images work to influence and shape environmental knowl-edge. The third aspect noted the need to identify connections across stories, places and histories if we are to begin to understand how media work within environmental debate to potentially engage publics in the environment as an issue, and crisis. The importance of this is shown by the surge in media space given over to a new category, 'the environment', across much of the industri-alized world in the late 1960s, while also recognizing the nuances that existed in different localities and nations around the histories and understandings of 'the environment'. The fourth point was 'the environment' that is the subject of mediated public debate is constructed through complex processes of knowledge transfer, reflexive interactions, meaning making and symbolic interplay, where conflict, power and emotions are also engaged, and we need to become highly attuned to these processes and 'pulls' if we are to better understand media roles in environmental debate. This is evident through every example presented above. In order to untan-gle the complexity of processes, practices and interconnections involved in the relationship between media and environmental debate, these themes are all revisited throughout the book. That media have long played a profound role in the construction and communication of knowledge about environmental concerns and risks is clear. The aim now is to reveal features and dynamics behind this role.

2

Conflict and Risk

Every battle we fight is a battle for the hearts and minds of other people. The only chance we have of reaching people who haven't yet heard what we've got to say is through the media. We might, with good reason, regard the papers and broadcasters with extreme suspicion, we might feel cheapened and compromised by engaging with them. But the war we're fighting is an information war, and we have to use all the weapons at our disposal. Whether we use the media or not, our opponents will. However just our cause and true our aims, they will use it to demonize and demolish us, unless we fight back. Exploit the media, or they will exploit you! (George Monbiot, 'An Activists' Guide to Exploiting the Media')

In his well accessed guide, UK activist and media columnist George Monbiot reveals how important it is to get into the news (2002). No news presence, he clearly recognizes, condemns political messages and their sponsors to obscurity and insecurity. But what Monbiot's useful, hardline and – for journalists – undoubtedly uncomfortable guide also reveals is the conflict inherent in the relationship between political challengers and media, and its complexity. Media variously become an opportunity, a target, a gatekeeper, the enemy, a game and an arena. For Monbiot, they are a space determined by economics, ideology and professional practices with a narrow concept of fairness, and filled with weak and cowardly individuals with short attention spans and a shared reluctance to upset their bosses – who will, nevertheless, respond well to an atmosphere of secrecy, excitement and intrigue. 'All journalists love to imagine they're in the Famous Five,' Monbiot writes. 'Be very nice to them and make them think they're part of the gang.'

Monbiot's guide is an explicit articulation of the concerns and difficulties faced by activists and other non-elite political challengers, but also – more broadly – all those wanting to be seen or heard. Visibility is necessary to participate in public debate and the principal way to achieve this is through media. Getting into the media can be difficult in itself, staying there even harder. Most difficult of all is achieving ongoing positive representation. For Monbiot, it is a kind of game, in which many of the participants are not told the rules. Nevertheless, 'If you don't play by the rules, it's a foul and you're sent off. As our only objective is to win, regardless of etiquette, we tend to foul more often than other contributors'.

Who plays and how are important concerns, and ones central to democratic anxieties about news media roles and responsibilities in public debate and engagement. They raise questions about access to the public sphere, and how voices are heard and messages circulated; about how environmental problems emerge as issues onto the public agenda to be debated, negotiated and subsequently acted upon; and about how people come together and publics form in response to and in order to respond to environmental and other crises, concerns and risks. To consider these questions, this chapter brings together a range of interconnected approaches and concepts through a lens focused on environmental conflict: the first relates to the popular notion of a public domain or sphere where ideas are openly exchanged and debated; the second engages with the theorization of a public arena as a limited space and in which social problems must compete for visibility; the third draws on work from the growing area of mediated conflict studies, which helps to conceptualize the means by which challengers participate – albeit on an uneven field – in social and political conflict; and the fourth shows how Ulrich Beck's risk society thesis provides an important site for considering the role of media in the staging of such conflicts, while also leading to the formation of publics that increasingly cross national and geographic boundaries to possibly address environmental crises and concerns. Together, these approaches help explain the conditions that allow and prevent different voices from being heard within public debate on the environment, conditions that will be further elaborated upon in the next chapter when news practice is considered in greater detail.

Debating the environment

The concept of a public sphere has played an important part in contemporary theorizing on media roles and responsibilities in public debate. Its concern with the processes of opinion formation and possible subsequent political actions – about how a plurality of voices and positions can come together and be heard on an equal basis – provides a key to understanding environmental conflict, as well as a normative ambition for political debate. At its heart are questions about consensus and contest, access and equality, about how we practise politics – 'not as an elite occupation in which some of the public take part once every four or five years through elections, but as an ongoing process through which "active citizens" can help to shape both the ends and the means of a good society' (Edwards 2009: 68).

In its best known form, that devised by Jurgen Habermas in his *The Structural Transformation of the Public Sphere* (1962/1989), it is idealized as a space where people can come together – equally and freely – and deliberate on issues of public importance. As a space free of constraints, inducements or threats, debate should be thorough and decisions sound (Downey 2007: 118). Habermas locates this idealized if not fully achieved public sphere historically, in the coffee houses and salons of late seventeenth- and eighteenth-century Europe. Here, in Germany, France and England, the 'representative publicness' of the Middle Ages, where the powerful simply displayed their majesty and power to the public, was gradually replaced by a genuine exchange of ideas between the bourgeoisie and the aristocracy. The infant press was an integral part of this process (Conboy 2004: 56). However, for

Habermas, the bourgeois public sphere was short lived. By the mid-late nineteenth century, social changes including increased literacy resulting from industrialization and urbanization created a commercial vacuum that was filled by the popular press. A consequence of this was the gradual shift from a public comprising a limited group of informed citizens to a mass public of consumers, a public sphere in 'appearance only' (Habermas 1962/1989: 171). By the twentieth century, the public sphere had become a space dominated by elite political and economic actors, using their power to attempt to shape public opinion via the mass media. Advertising, entertainment and public relations had weakened journalism's critical role and public opinion was 'no longer a process of rational discourse but the result of publicity and social engineering in the media' (Dahlgren 1991: 4).

It is here with its reflection of contemporary anxieties about commercialism of the media and their exposure to potential manipulation via in part their increasing reliance on promotional material that the relevance of Habermas' early theorizing for modern mass communication research becomes clear (Manning 2001: 9). But it is also the conceptualization of a liberal public sphere in decline as a result of a commercial popular mass media that has been most criticized. For example, James Curran writes that Habermas' analysis is 'stimulating and thought-provoking', but deeply flawed (1991: 46). 'It is based on contrasting a golden era that never existed with an equally misleading representation of present times as a dystopia. The contrast does not survive empirical historical scrutiny.'

Several foci of this debate are especially relevant to analysis of media roles in environmental conflict. One is concerned with the conceptualization of the public sphere as comprising individual citizens making representations on their own behalf rather than, as is more common in modern politics, represented by interest groups or political parties (Curran 2002: 233; Stevenson 2002: 71). Contemporary environmental debate is dominated by groups and organizations, formal and informal, with structures and spokespeople representing their members, whether citizens with environmental concerns, companies, scientific organizations or governments. The individual citizen, as will be discussed in Chapter Four, may participate in mediated environmental debate, but often within strict parameters. A second focus is on the marginalization of alternative or competing spheres, such as those created by women, and the exclusive nature of the bourgeois public sphere (see, for example, Fraser 1992: 122–3; Schudson 2003: 69), again drawing comparison with contemporary environmental debate where peripheral political and social actors, as well as other interested parties such as scientists or farmers, are coming together to exchange ideas and compete to have their voices heard. Habermas has also been accused of underestimating the level of turbulence and change in the public sphere, particularly during times of crisis (Downey 2007: 118). This dynamism, according to John Downey, is created by several factors: the contradictory values of the public sphere – liberal universalist on the one hand, dominated by those with political and/or economic power on the other; by the fact that journalists and even political elites themselves will look more broadly for answers if elites are unable to solve a crisis; and that counter-publics, such as marginalized sections of the environment movement, are able to use protest and other forms of 'dramaturgical self-presentation' to influence elites and political decision making (2007: 119).

A final relevant focus of debate is on the concept of refeudalization. How convincing is the connection of the perceived focus on celebrity and promotion in contemporary politics to that of the 'representative publicness' of the Middle Ages? According to John B. Thompson (1995: 75), any similarity is more apparent than real. He writes that 'the development of communication media has created new forms of interaction, new kinds of visibility and new networks of information diffusion in the modern world, all of which have altered the symbolic character of social life so profoundly that any comparison between mediated politics today and the theatrical practices of feudal courts is superficial at best' (1995: 75). Publics formed by television, for example, differ from those formed by face-to-face communications in fundamental ways: actions and events are visible today to a far greater number of people; television viewers may see places far from their own, although others control their field of vision; and viewers remain invisible to the individuals who appear before them on their televisions (Thompson 1995: 129–30). These differences point to the production of a new kind of visibility – that is, new ways of being seen or heard by others.

The rise of the internet and its move from a few-to-many to a many-to-many communication model has necessarily shifted analytical focus in recent years. Certainly, the internet has been a tantalizing source of hope for environmental activists since the 1990s, offering potential for independent information distribution devoid of the mediating effect of news journalists and established news media industries (Rucht 2004: 55). However, we should be wary of too quickly celebrating the new emancipatory potential of the internet. As Downey notes, the internet is less 'one big piazza' where citizens produce as well as consume news and opinion and non-elite political actors can impact public opinion and policy, and more a 'a useful tool for counter-publics in order to regroup and train for agitation and to engage in counter-publicity' (2007: 115–16). Realistically, in order for counter-publicity to be successful, 'it has to breach the walls of the mass media public sphere and be carried to those who either are internet disconnected or politically disenfranchised' (Downey 2007: 118).

Recent research is showing how environmental activists and organizations are using the internet less as a direct means of garnering support and public opinion or influencing decision makers, and more as a way to attract the attention of and communicate with news journalists (Lester and Hutchins 2009; Hutchins and Lester 2010), research that will be discussed in detail in Chapter Five in relation to protest. Likewise, celebrity is being deployed by political challengers in and through news media, and in complex and evolving ways that recognize both its capacity to influence debate and its limits, as will be shown in Chapter Six. The important point here is that while the rapidly changing nature of mediated communications in environmental politics means the roles of 'old' and 'new' media, and the relationship between the two, are still evolving, the question of access to the public sphere remains highly pertinent. As Thompson writes:

The public domain itself has become a complex space of information flows in which words, images and symbolic content compete for attention as individuals and organizations seek to make themselves seen and heard (or to make others be seen and heard). This is a space that is shaped not only by the constantly changing technologies that enable words and images to be recorded and transmitted to distant others, but also by the institutions and organizations that have an interest in transmitting this content (or not, as the case may be) and that have differing quantities of power and resources to pursue their aims. To achieve visibility through the media is to gain a kind of presence or recognition in the public space, which can help to call attention to one's situation or to advance one's cause. But equally, the inability to achieve visibility through the media can confine one to obscurity – and in the worst cases, can lead to a kind of death by neglect. Hence it is not surprising that *struggles for visibility* have come to assume such significance in our societies today. Mediated visibility is not just a vehicle through which aspects of social and political life are brought to the attention of others: it has become a principal means by which social and political struggles are articulated and carried out. (Thompson 2005: 49, original emphasis)

It is to explicit conceptualizations of this competition for limited space in the public domain that the chapter now turns.

Public arenas

As we have seen, 1969 was a good year for the environment in the media. 'The environment' developed into an issue in its own right, rather than a series of disparate and disconnected problems, and a contemporary environment movement emerged around the Western world with not only a clear understanding of the importance of media coverage to their cause, but conditioned towards gaining the attention of media through their activities, strategies and even leadership. By the early 1970s, however, this attention was much harder to achieve, and coverage had again splintered. Another good year was 1988. Here again 'the environment' found a central place in news and other media. By 1991 and the first Gulf War, however, the issue was again in decline. The most recent surge of interest occurred in 2004–5, from which climate change finally emerged as a recognized crisis, but by early 2010, opinion polls were finding that this too was slipping down the rankings of issues considered to require urgent priority attention (Pew Research Centre 2010) and governments around the world began backtracking from policy commitments. Marked by such volatility, the environment provides a compelling site of analysis for those attempting to understand why and how issues enter the public domain, only to again exit. That the environment has emerged most recently as a crisis of global proportions calling out for urgent action and yet still undergoes such a fall from the public agenda makes it all the more important that such analysis is performed.

Anthony Downs' 'Up and Down with Ecology – the "Issue-Attention Cycle"' was published in 1972, before the full extent of that first 'down' was being realized in the United States. His cycle identifies five stages, which he claims will vary in duration depending on the issue involved but will almost always occur in the same sequence (1972: 39–41). The first is the pre-problem stage. While the problem exists and some experts and groups may be alarmed by it, it has not yet captured the public attention. Objective conditions are usually far worse at this stage than they are by the time the public becomes interested in it. The second stage is marked by 'alarmed discovery and euphoric enthusiasm'. The public becomes aware of and alarmed by the problem, perhaps as a result of a dramatic series of events. This is invariably accompanied by enthusiasm for American society's capacity to quickly solve the problem. Realizing the cost of significant progress is the third stage. Here, the costs – both financial and others – of fixing the issue intervene and the public realizes also that it may in fact be beneficiaries of the continuing problem. For example, cars cause traffic congestion and smog (and, we might now add, carbon emissions) but remain desirable if not essential for most. Gradual decline of intense public interest follows. The public may feel discouraged, threatened and/or bored, and consequently efforts to keep the problem on the public agenda decline.

Also, at this stage, another novel problem is entering stage two. Finally comes the post-problem stage, where issues enter a state of 'prolonged limbo', although they now have a different relation to public attention than they did while in the pre-problem stage. For example, new institutions, programs and policies may have been put into place that persist despite a lack of public attention. Downs suggests that problems that have been through the issue-attention cycle will, on average, achieve more prominence overall than those which are still in the pre-discovery stage.

While prescient in its prediction that the environment would suffer a gradual but not complete loss of public attention and useful in its conceptualization of the reflexive relationship between media and the public, Downs' model can take us only so far towards an understanding of issues in the public domain. This is primarily because of the model's representation of the journey of issues as linear, orderly and distinct, with little acknowledgement of the potential for interaction between issues. Likewise, Downs puts the initial rise in concern down to widespread awareness of environmental deterioration – such as pollution or oil spills – rather than because of successful strategy by claims makers or institutional action in the highly contested space that is the public sphere. William Solesbury's attempt to explain how some environmental situations become political issues that demand responses from government is clear that any model that represents the process as 'linear, staged, sequential or single-stranded would be an oversimplification' (1976: 396). According to Solesbury, an environmental issue must pass at least one of three tests: to command attention, to claim legitimacy and/or to invoke action. A failure to pass all three would remove the issue from the agenda completely (1976: 395), but passing one may be enough to bring it to government notice. For example, an issue may command attention in the media and, even if nothing is done in response, there may be a growth in support. Changing circumstances – new crises, further cases or fresh campaigns – may also maintain the issue's legitimacy. While recognizing a greater level of complexity and influences on the 'careers' of environmental issues, Solesbury's focus is on institutional factors, less so on professional practices and cultural influences, and thus his capacity to elaborate on the dynamics behind the complexity is also limited. For a model that ranges across these diverse features but remains nevertheless nuanced in its consideration of how social problems rise and fall, we can turn to Stephen Hilgartner and Charles L. Bosk's still influential public arenas model (1988).

Here the focus is on interactions *among* problems. Hilgartner and Bosk emphasize the competition that occurs within public arenas between social problems, which they stress are socially constructed and projections of collective sentiment, rather than 'simple mirrors of objective conditions of society' (1988: 53–4). A large population of social problem claims competes within institutional arenas for attention and growth. Hilgartner and Bosk develop a set of theoretical propositions over several levels for untangling the complexities of how and why social problems emerge and disappear from public debate. They highlight:

1. a dynamic process of competition among the members of a very large 'population' of social problem claims;
2. institutional arenas that serve as 'environments' where social problems compete for attention and grow;
3. 'carrying capacities' of these arenas, which limit the number of problems that can gain widespread attention at one time;
4. 'principles of selection', or institutional, political and cultural factors that influence the probability of survival of competing problem formulations;
5. patterns of interaction among the different arenas, such as feedback and synergy, through which activities in each arena spread throughout the others; and
6. networks of operatives who promote and attempt to control particular problems and whose channels of communication crisscross the different arenas. (Hilgartner and Bosk 1988: 56)

This is acknowledgement of the contingent nature of a multitude of influences, an 'ecological' approach for thinking about social problems and the public arena. It becomes a space where drama, novelty, symbolic interplays, reflexive interactions and relationships, institutional logics, competition and strategic actions all play a part. Hilgartner and Bosk have criticized earlier models such as Downs' for focusing on single problems and their struggles for attention, arguing that many problems exist simultaneously in several stages of development, and 'patterns of progression from one stage to the next vary sufficiently to question the claim that a typical career exists' (1988: 54–5). Public attention, they argue, is a scarce resource, and as such the success of a problem can be measured by the attention it receives in a range of arenas (1988: 53). Social problems can rise and fall in a number of public arenas at once, in which case synergies and feedback between arenas contribute to that growth and decline (1988: 67).

The authors list a wide variety of public arenas, including government, the courts, movies, social action groups, books dealing with social issues, and news media. 'It is in these institutions that social problems are discussed, selected, defined, framed, dramatized, packaged, and presented to the public' (Hilgartner and Bosk 1988: 59). They contend that the carrying capacities of arenas are finite, and that as a result, there is fierce competition between social problems for entry into each arena and onto the public agenda (1988: 70). Nuclear energy, ozone depletion and climate change are among the environmental problems that have been studied in relation to Hilgartner and Bosk's model (see, for example, Mazur 1990; Joppke 1991; Ungar 1998; McGaurr and Lester 2009). These studies agree that issues not only compete for public attention but can also help carry each other into the public arena, thus raising further complexities about the finite or otherwise carrying capacities of arenas and stressing the danger of viewing social problems in isolation. 'Since problems from a similar domain (like the environment) often appear in batches and benefit from their common presence, studies of individual social problems are likely to miss or distort key processes,' Ungar writes (1998: 513).

The debate over nuclear power and climate change in Australia illustrates some of the complexities faced when attempting to identify the processes whereby environmental issues compete for recognition as social problems (McGaurr and Lester 2009). In mid-2006, climate change was frequently called into service by the then prime minister John Howard as justification for, at the very least, a debate as to whether Australia should turn to nuclear energy. However, early in this debate, nuclear energy was often represented in the *Australian* newspaper as a problem with environmental characteristics and risks. By February 2007, after the release of a number of high-profile reports and further cementation of climate change as a crisis, the situation was very different. The *Australian* approached nuclear energy as a technological issue, rarely including any mention of its environmental risks. While it appears that in May 2006 nuclear energy and climate change were sub-categories of the macro-problem of environmental risk, by February 2007 they had decidedly distinct characteristics. Nuclear energy was now being framed as a technological solution to climate change. Moreover, the fact that most articles about nuclear energy also included a mention of climate change suggests that climate change was helping significantly to keep the nuclear energy issue alive. The conditions under which issues may compete for attention or indeed ease each other's paths into the public arena clearly cannot be separated from the processes which lead to the formation of issue frames and their shifts across time. An approach that recognizes the level of conflict within the public sphere – conflict that may lead to the formation of a collective vision, or not – is better equipped to identify such conditions and processes, and to ask how these interconnect.

Mediated conflict

While much conflict continues to exist outside the media arena – for example, personal and professional conflict – those conflicts seeking to prompt public and political response need in almost every case to be mediated to some degree. As we have seen, a sometimes 'brutal war of words and images' and 'struggles to be seen and heard' have become an 'inseparable part of the social and political conflicts of our time' (Thompson 2005: 49). I want to outline here a general approach for thinking about media and conflict, and identify key themes to which we need to stay attuned when we turn specifically to the environment. This approach – underlying the work, notably, of Wolfsfeld (1997) and Cottle (2006) – recognizes the complexities and confluence of factors at work, including media ownership and regulation, institutional traditions and organizational logics, professional practices, and symbolic and other cultural interplays; a mix that acknowledges questions of power and inequalities within the media sphere without denying the level of turbulence, challenge, conflict and change that is also possible. Not only possible, but actual. Every day stories find their way into the news that challenge social norms and economic might, that advocate environmental change, that insist on political action.

As noted earlier, in their principal focus on political and economic power, some attempts to explain environmental coverage are unable to satisfactorily deal with the presence of these stories. Nevertheless, to ignore the impact of such concentrations of power would also leave explanations of media and political conflict clearly lacking (Cottle 2006: 20). Perhaps the most influential account of how media work to perpetuate inequalities and silence peripheral political and social actors via their economic and elite connections is provided by Edward Herman and Noam Chomsky's *Manufacturing Consent: The Political Economy of the Mass Media* (1988). The mass media, it argues:

> serve as a system for communicating messages and symbols to the general populace. It is their function to amuse, entertain, and inform, and to inculcate individuals with the values, beliefs, and codes of behaviour that will integrate them into the institutional structures of the larger society. In a world of concentrated wealth and major conflicts of class interest, to fulfil this role requires systematic propaganda. (Herman and Chomsky 1988: 1)

Their 'propaganda model' focuses on this inequality of wealth and power in the United States 'and its multilevel effects on mass-media interests and choices'. They propose five essential reasons or 'filters': one, the size, ownership and profit orientation of media companies; two, advertising as the primary source of media income; three, the reliance of media on information provided by government, business and 'experts' funded by government and business; four, 'flak' – or a process of negative feedback and response – as a primary means of disciplining media; and five, 'anti-communism' as a national religion and control mechanism (1988: 3–30). Together, these filters work to 'narrow the range of news that passes through the gates', leading to a dichotomization that is both massive and systematic: 'not only are the choices for publicity and suppression comprehensible in terms of system advantage, but the modes of handling favoured and inconvenient materials (placement, tone, context, fullness of treatment) differ in ways that serve political ends' (1988: 35).

The model is important for its highlighting of issues of ownership and profits, which have seen many news organizations cut newsroom staff and therefore their capacity to cover a range of issues, including the environment, in depth; for its recognition of the vulnerability of news organizations to powerful interests via their reliance on advertising and access to information generated by these interests; and its focus on underlying ideologies and discourses, which can frame media coverage in ways that are not immediately obvious. When considering environmental coverage, we might replace 'anti-communism' with 'economic growth', for example. Yet, it cannot explain how so many stories countering the power of these controlling interests do find their way into media, how journalists and news organizations act in ways to reveal what such interests would rather keep hidden or to counter 'flak', and how audiences may interpret and understand such coverage. As later chapters address such issues in relation to environmental coverage, criticism of the 'manufacturing consent' model is worth considering here as it highlights where we can fruitfully look for more nuanced explanations. For Michael Schudson, a stance that places the *New York Times* and *Pravda*, the official newspaper of the Soviet Union, together as vehicles of propaganda is 'misleading and mischievous' (2003: 38). While US journalists may be American patriots, this and other news positions are rarely dictated to them by their employers. There is also a legitimate arena of political controversy in the United States and despite 'foreshortening' the representation of the views of the left, multiple voices appear in the American news media. Schudson also argues that the US media need to both make profits *and* maintain credibility. Together, these complicate Herman and Chomsky's 'extremely critical' view (Schudson 2003: 40). For Brian McNair (2006: 37–41), Herman and Chomsky exaggerate and decontextualize the bias of media content, overgeneralizing the impact of the content of some media organizations, and understating the level and impact of exceptions. The Watergate affair and the savage media criticism of the Vietnam War are two examples of 'exceptions' that had substantial political consequences, yet are explained away (McNair 2006: 37). For Simon Cottle, the propaganda model provides a 'formidable critique' of media involvement in the processes of manufacturing consent and how they may be subservient to 'important levers of economic and political power', yet is ultimately 'unnerving' in its generalizing, almost conspiratorial, tone and economic reductionism, and lack of engagement with changing dynamics, contests and contradictions that occur between and within centres of power (2006: 17–20).

More useful approaches may vary in the weight they put on institutional, organizational and professional activities and broader social and cultural contexts, as well as the effects of economic and political power, but they are unified in avoiding placing journalists and news sources within a static field or fields isolated from others and rigidly delineated. Gadi Wolfsfeld's *Media and Political Conflict: News from the Middle East* (1997) can serve to highlight many of their interests. For Wolfsfeld, the media constitute an arena on which battles for political influence are fought, structurally and culturally. There is the main gate for those regarded as 'exceptionally eminent' and a rear gate intended for the 'exceptionally weird' (1997: 20). But once in, through whichever gate, the struggle becomes one about meaning and is 'more than a simple test of raw force' (1997: 55).

Wolfsfeld's model contends that the best approach for understanding the role of the news media in political conflict is to consider the 'competition over the news media as part of a more general contest for political control' (1997: 197). He also argues that the role of news media in a conflict can be measured by the nature and extent of adaptation by various antagonists; the weaker the antagonist the more pronounced the changes in tactics, strategy and behaviour will be (1997: 65–6). Control of the political environment rests on three factors: the ability to initiate and control events, the ability to regulate the flow of information, and the ability to mobilize elite support. Variables in the level of control allow challengers to compete (1997: 250). The logistic and geographic environment also affects the ability of the powerful to regulate the flow of information and thus control the political environment. 'While the physical circumstances of certain locales facilitate government control, other locations are more porous and offer easier access for reporters, thereby increasing the level of journalistic independence' (Wolfsfeld 1997: 28).

Overall, Wolfsfeld finds there are two major factors that set important limits on the ability of authorities to totally dominate media frames:

> The first is that they often lose control over the political environment and this offers important opportunities for challengers to promote alternative frames to the press. Secondly, there are many influences within the professional and political culture of the news media that work against the authorities. Those challengers who can overcome the obstacles of entrance to the central arena will be given a genuine opportunity to fight. (Wolfsfeld 1997: 49)

This acknowledgement that, despite an uneven playing field, challengers are able to at least join the game and impact on framing of an issue is vital and helps explain the broad range of conditions that influence and shape media coverage of the environment. Here, media become both the arena on which the battle for social change is fought, and a player. Sources also play a complicated, multi-faceted role. However, before turning in more detail to these journalistic and source roles, we need to widen our focus even further, and consider the broader political and social landscapes in which they function and the publics and networks that form through and around them. While the work of social theorists Anthony Giddens and Manuel Castells, in their conceptualizations of reflexive modernization and the network society as well in more recent books (Castells 2009; Giddens 2009), have much to offer in the study of media and environmental conflict, I want to concentrate here on the influential work of Ulrich Beck, as he suggests media play a profound role in the awareness and communication of environmental danger, and in bringing individuals together to respond.

Risk society

On 1 August 2009, the *Sydney Morning Herald* published a plea from fifteen of Australia's leading climate scientists in the form of a letter to the editor. The scientists warned that the threat from climate change was 'real, urgent and approaching a series of "tipping points"' where it would feed on itself. Yet, despite 'more serious' assessments of the risk, climate change deniers were reappearing with increasing regularity in the Australian debate. According to a news story relating to the letter:

> Dr Raupach, who monitors greenhouse gas emissions globally, said the scientists joined together because of their growing concern about climate scepticism in the Australian debate. 'It's a concern that I think is widely felt among many climate scientists in Australia,' he said. He referred to sceptics' claims that the earth was cooling and that solar flares and sunspots were responsible for increasing warming, not human-caused emissions from burning fossil fuels and cutting down forests. 'These arguments keep being recycled even though they have been rebutted in public many times,' Dr Raupach said. 'We felt the need to state the evidence-based position as we see it.' (Wilkinson 2009)

Here are scientists struggling for visibility, for their views to be provided with more credibility within public debate, their definitions and assessments of risk to be privileged. That this has not occurred automatically – and, in fact, has remained quite elusive in the debate over climate change in Australia – has forced scientists to join other environmental and risk claims makers to effectively 'stage' their risk claims to the public via media.

In his earlier writings, *Risk Society* (1992) and *World Risk*

Society (1999), as in his more recent treatises, *The Cosmopolitan Vision* (2006) and *World at Risk* (2009), Ulrich Beck grants media and especially television a central role in maintaining both public knowledge and public anxiety about risk. Such a role is now enacted in an increasingly global forum, and across global networks, further complicating the histories and dynamics of conflicts, and the collective sentiments and local actions that result. What this means, according to Beck, is 'that it is increasingly difficult to make a clear and binding distinction between hysteria and deliberate fear-mongering, on the one hand, and appropriate fear and precaution, on the other' (Beck 2009: 12).

For Beck, the 'organized irresponsibility' that results from a disconnect between risk and responsibility in this period of modernity leaves no-one to blame and everyone to blame, and is thus a major issue in most of the political conflicts of our times (1995: 58–69, 1999: 6). Here, we are all both perpetrators of environmental harm – when we drive our cars or use electricity generated by coal, for example – and victims. Moreover, as risks become larger in scale, even global, decision makers become less equipped to assess their dangers and or to prevent their growth. At the same time, the sciences no longer have a monopoly on rationality, instead becoming 'product and producer of reality and problems which they are to analyse and overcome' and, as such, 'targeted not only as a source of solutions to problems, but also as a *cause of problems*' (Beck 1992: 156, original emphasis). What counts as proof, Beck also asks, 'in a world where knowledge and lack of knowledge of risks are inextricably fused and knowledge is contested and probabilistic?' (2009: 320).

Beck repeatedly acknowledges the centrality of media in the circulation, contestation and interpretation of knowledge about environmental risk. Indeed, he says that risk society – or societies that are 'confronted by the challenges of the self-created possibility, hidden at first, then increasingly apparent, of the self-destruction of all life on this earth' (1995: 67) – can only be understood if one starts from the premise that it is always also 'a knowledge, media and information society at the same time' (2000: xiv). 'Relations of definition' determine who defines the harmfulness of products and what kind of proof is required, circulated and counts; they inform and frame mediated knowledge of environmental risks and hazards while also being informed and framed themselves by media (Allan et al. 2000: 2, 14). The existence of risks, Beck writes, 'takes the form of (scientific and alternative scientific) knowledge':

> As a result their 'reality' can be dramatized or minimized, transformed or simply denied according to the norms which decide what is known and what is not. They are products of struggles and conflicts over definitions within the context of specific relations of definitional power, hence the (in varying degrees successful) results of staging. (Beck 2009: 30)

As such, media have become an arena where ordinary voices, including Beck's so-called 'voices of the side effects', also compete for attention and challenge 'organized irresponsibility'; where political activism and citizen actions are played out not on the street but on television; where 'the accumulated bad conscience of the actors and consumers of industrial society can be offloaded'; and where cultural symbols are 'staged' (Beck 1996: 22). However, media do not have free rein to construct environmental problems as serious issues. They are restrained by a range of factors, including public relations activities and other forms of damage control, which Beck calls the 'dance of the veiling of the hazards'.

It is symbolic power that allows media to take on a vital role in the illumination of these hazards, which are 'not merely projected on the world stage, but really threaten' (1995: 101):

> Herein lies a crucial limitation of direct politics. Human beings are like children wandering around in a 'forest of symbols' (Baudelaire). In other words, we have to rely on the symbolic politics of the media. This holds especially because of the abstractness and omnipresence of destruction which keep the world risk society going. Tangible, simplifying symbols, in which cultural nerve fibres are touched and alarmed, here take on central political importance. These symbols have to be produced or forged in the open fire of conflict provocation, before the strained and terrified public of television viewers. The key question is: Who discovers (or invents), and how, symbols that disclose the

structural character of the problems while at the same time fostering the ability to act? (Beck 2009: 98)

While Beck, more than many contemporary social theorists, locates media centrally in his writings, he has largely left the work of describing their role in any empirical detail to other researchers. Cottle describes Beck's 'world risk society' formulation as profound, but identifies a seeming 'slippage between ontological statements about the reality of "risks" and epistemological claims about how we come to know about them' (Cottle 2006: 123). The interplay of the nuclear energy and climate change problems in Australia – mentioned earlier – helps to briefly illustrate some of Beck's concerns but also Cottle's point (McGaurr and Lester 2009). On the face of it, the evolution of the problem of climate change as represented by media could be considered evidence that society is moving from the organized irresponsibility of late modernity towards Beck's vision of a global civil society whose first obligation is to humanity and the planet (Beck 1999: 17–18). However, as scientific certainty and public concern about the risks of climate change increased in Australia between 2004 and 2006, both the government and media found in climate change a reason to ramp up attention to nuclear energy while playing down its potential risk. This was a turn of events not only perfectly aligned with Beck's description of modernity's faith in the ability of technology to overcome the hazards technology itself creates, but hints at the contradictions and complications involved in media roles in both constructing and unveiling environmental risks.

A feature of Beck's risk society thesis is its emphasis on individualization and new forms of politics. Paradoxically, just as individuals are set free from the restraints of industrial society, including class stratification, family and gender status, their capacity to act as individuals against risks is diminished because of the diffuse form of contemporary risks, such as climate change (Hannigan 2006: 24). For Beck, however, this is the key to the formation of social movements and citizen's groups; that in the desire for a 'life of one's own' individuals will work collectively to break down social or political barriers to achieve that desire. Thus, on the one hand, new social movements are 'expressions of the new risk situations in the risk society. On the other, they result from the search for social and personal identities and commitments in detraditionalized culture' (Beck 1992: 90). Risk brings people together as publics. For Beck, this is risk's essential feature, what it actually does; it creates 'a public by promoting public awareness of risk' (2006: 34), and that public is increasingly global in nature. A 'globalization of emotions and empathy' can occur when publics emerge from the knowledge of risk, and the media play a critical role in allowing people to experience themselves as parts of a 'fragmented, endangered civilization and civil society characterized by the simultaneity of events and knowledge of this simultaneity all over the world' (Beck 2006: 42). There can be powerful political outcomes, as the 'more ubiquitous the threat as represented in the mass media, the greater the political power to explode borders generated by the perception of risk' (Beck 2006: 35). This:

> *forces* people to communicate with one another in spite of themselves, and forces a public into existence where it is supposed to be prevented. It allocates duties and costs to those who decline them (often with the backing of valid laws). In other words, risks explode self-referential systems and national and international political agendas, overturning their priorities and producing practical interconnections among mutually indifferent or hostile parties and camps. (Beck 2006: 36, original emphasis)

Here, important questions are raised about media roles in the formation of publics that are willing and able to engage in environmental issues. Understanding connections between media, environmental risk, everyday lives and geopolitical boundaries and how such connections can prompt or stifle a willingness and capacity for ordinary people and decision makers to act is a key challenge for media researchers and, indeed, all those concerned about the environment. Increasingly, such questions are being asked in a globalized setting; where cosmopolitanism and environmental citizenship connect with problems and risks that are planted firmly in the local and flow effortlessly across national and geographic boundaries; how public opinion and decision making is shaped when local and national boundaries become less meaningful and/or are strategically breached in order to find and mobilize international support and pressure. We also need to consider questions of public empathy and response to distant concerns and crises. These concerns will be returned to in the final chapter. Beforehand, however, we need to focus more closely on media themselves. For George Monbiot (2002), the key to successful political challenge is a clear understanding of the logic of media organizations, the political and economic pressures within which they operate, and the professional practices of journalists. He recognizes rightly that these are central to political conflict and risk recognition. Likewise, for the Australian climate scientists, an understanding of news practices could help explain the re-emergence of climate change denial claims within the crucial public debate. As such, it is to news media that the next chapter turns.

3

News and Journalists

> If you think of readers of a newspaper as consumers, they need to feel as though the story is relevant to their lives, that it's going to have some impact on them. So sometimes it's very hard to convince editors [of] an environmental problem, which is going to start to have an impact in fifty to 100 years. It's very hard to sell that. Basically until the editors think that the water from rising sea levels is going to be lapping on the front door of people's houses, then it's pretty hard to convince them to be interested in the story. (James Woodford, former environment reporter, *Sydney Morning Herald*, 2002)

The environment, more than many issues, brings to the surface some of the most persistent anxieties surrounding news media practices: the limited capacity of journalism to take a long-term view; the arbitrary nature of values and norms used to determine newsworthiness; restricted information gathering, source access and forms of story-telling; the role of journalists as 'objective' reporters of facts or advocates for action and change. Such concerns are sharpened when news media are confronted with the environment as an issue and forced to grapple with its complexities, histories and meanings, and the range of voices and views battling to be heard, and it is an issue on which they are often deemed to comprehensively fail. The reason for their failure, in the eyes of some critics and with echoes of the 'manufacturing consent' paradigm considered in the previous chapter, is relatively straightforward: the producers of news – the owners, editors, reporters – are aligned with society's economically powerful, whether actually through ownership or through a chain of like-mindedness and shared interests and ambitions. Sharon Beder, for example, writes that corporate ownership of the media clearly influences environmental reporting, 'especially when it comes to issues such as dioxin which have such large and immediate financial ramifications for media owners' (2000: 230). She continues that while the media are also influenced by news sources, 'the corporate agenda of the large media moguls is not so different from that of their corporate advertisers'.

> News is defined firstly by those who have privileged access to the media as sources and interpreters – public relations people, government officials and accredited experts. It is then shaped according to journalistic conventions, aimed at attracting and entertaining an audience for advertisers, and fitted into a general framework and approach that suits corporate owners. All these influences determine the news output that most people depend on for information about the world beyond their personal experience. (Beder 2000: 230–1)

Such accounts, as noted previously, serve to turn our attention towards issues of ownership and the power of sources. They also usefully reflect public anxiety about media roles, practices and values, and media fulfilment or otherwise of what is widely perceived as their responsibilities. But, in the main, they fail to acknowledge the complexity and changing dynamics of media practices. While they clearly recognize the conflict that exists between media and the less powerful sections of society, they do not recognize the level of competition that exists between media and elite sources, or indeed within and between media themselves and within and between various elite organizations and institutions. This reduces the influences on news to a small if powerful handful, with shared ambitions that – intentionally or not – run counter to the environment's best interests.

The production of news is influenced by more, and this chapter's aim – through a lens focused on environmental coverage – is to begin to untangle some of the professional, organizational, institutional, cultural and other factors that impact on the production of news. It starts by extending the concept of social construction from the environment to news, which allows news to be understood as a deeply contested site where issues develop and agendas are set, before considering in some detail the professional values and practices behind environmental news production. It concludes by considering one of journalism's perennial anxieties. This is an anxiety that is openly debated in relation to coverage of the environment, if not in all areas of the profession; when does or should a journalist become an advocate? Should environmental journalists abandon objectivity as a central professional tenet? Would this better serve the public interest? These questions are asked in light of significant change that has affected news media, most notably in the form of the rise of the internet.

Constructing news

News has a confused relationship with reality. The metaphors of a mirror and reflection are not uncommonly heard in the professional discourses surrounding journalism (Allan 2004: 59; Zelizer 2004: 14). Exposing 'the facts', revealing 'the truth', these are surely what readers expect of news and what journalists work to deliver. Indeed, to be identified as news, every 35-centimetre newspaper story or 1.30 minute broadcast item should reveal something, provide some 'real' knowledge. However, it is important to recognize that the nature of this knowledge is open; open to debate, to interpretation, to shifting meanings, and thus often to vehement conflict. Acknowledging the competition that takes place around knowledge helps explain why news is such a contested space and to uncover further details of that contest.

Take this example: on 27 May 2006, the *New York Times* ran a story on indigenous claims to continue hunting polar bears. It included this statement: 'Other experts see a healthier population. They note that there are more than 20,000 polar bears roaming the Arctic, compared to as few as 5,000 40 years ago . . .' (Krauss 2006). Danish economist Bjorn Lomborg quoted this figure in the introduction to his influential book, *Cool It: The Skeptical Environmentalist's Guide to Global Warming* (2007: 3–9). From here, Peter Dykstra, CNN's executive producer of science, tech and weather, began following the trail as the 'fact' was repeated in various news and other media outlets; albeit often with some variations to numbers or time span. And continues to be repeated, as in this example from the *Wall Street Journal*: 'Nearly everyone agrees that there are more polar bears now than when scientists first started counting: Estimates put the population between 20,000 and 25,000, up from several thousand 50 years ago' (Dvorak 2009). The 'fact' also became a particular favourite of anti-anthropogenic global warming columnists and bloggers. When approached by Dykstra, *New York Times* reporter Clifford Krauss, who wrote the original story, could not recall the source of the 5,000 number, 'but said that he understood it to be "widely accepted"' (Dykstra 2008: 5). Meanwhile, a UK *Daily Telegraph* story was cited in a *Los Angeles Times* opinion piece – again stating that polar bear numbers had quadrupled – as confirming 'the ongoing polar bear population explosion'. The *Daily Telegraph* story, in fact, had noted only that there was strong population growth in one local population, while reporting global warming-related declines in another local population, and did not mention the 5,000-to-20,000 jump. Dykstra then tracked down scientists involved in measuring population numbers forty years ago, none of whom recalled the 5,000 estimate. The 'guesstimate', they claimed, was closer to 20–25,000 at the time. Dystkra concluded that the overall population of polar bears may have increased due to bans on hunting and other protection measures put in place in the 1950s–70s, mitigating to some extent the effects of climate change, but certainly not four or five-fold. In the end, there were no clear 'facts' on the population health of these well camouflaged and wide roaming bears. While an extreme example of news' uneasy relationship to reality, the 'evolution' of the polar bears story clearly shows how news is both constructed by a complex set of processes – whether professional, historical or ideological, to name just a few possible influences – and then constructs another version of reality itself. Polar bears may be elusive. More so is reality in news.

Brian McNair, in his conceptualization of news within a 'chaos' paradigm, puts it this way:

News is still what news always was: a socially constructed account of reality rather than reality itself, composed of literary, verbal and pictorial elements which combine to form a journalistic narrative disseminated through print, broadcast or online media. No matter how 'live' the news is, and regardless of how raw and visceral the account of events being brought into our living rooms appears to be, it is still a mediated version of reality. . . (McNair 2006: 6)

But, he continues, it is a mediated version of reality that:

when we receive it, and when we extend to it our trust in its authority as a representation of the real, transports us from the relative isolation of our domestic environments, the parochialism of our streets and small towns, the crowded bustle of our big cities, to memberships of virtual global communities, united in their access to *these* events, communally experienced at *this* moment, through global communication networks. (McNair 2006: 6, original emphasis)

In other words, news is a mediated version of reality but with significant and 'real' consequences.

Metaphors to explain news' relationship with the world abound. One of the most famous comes from Gaye Tuchman, who in her seminal *Making News* describes news as a 'window' on the world (1978: 1). She reminds us, however, that windows can distort the view: the angle and depth of vision will vary depending on where one is standing in a room; the view will vary depending on the clarity of the glass; the breadth of vision will vary depending on the window's size. For Tuchman, news is more than a mirror and a reflection of society and its interests. Instead, it actively contributes to the constitution of that society (1978: 184). Newsworkers are integral to these processes. For example, and of continuing relevance to environmental activism, Tuchman argues that stories about deviant actions do more than 'modify' the social structure. These stories, in fact, actively define both deviant and normative behaviour. News draws on embedded ideas and concerns, often failing to recognize how embedded it is itself in such societal concerns and institutions. 'It not only defines and redefines, constitutes and reconstitutes social meanings; it also defines and redefines, constitutes and reconstitutes ways of doing things – existing processes in existing institutions,' Tuchman claims (1978: 196). Here, then, news also becomes embedded in questions not only of knowledge and creativity, but of power. 'Telling stories of social life, news is a social resource. A source of knowledge, a source of power, news is a window on the world,' she concludes (1978: 217).

The number of polar bears in the world today as opposed to forty years ago was initially a powerful 'fact', not in its reflection of reality, but in how that 'fact' was constituted and what people did with it. It was a 'fact' with significant pedigree for circulation and action within the public sphere. It carried with it some credibility both for the journalist who produced the story and his readers; this power is provided by its scientific sources and historical comparative component, but also its connection with images of the lone polar bear in the threatened icy wilderness, a culturally resonating symbol of climate change risk. That its pedigree also included the legitimization that can come from an initial appearance in the *New York Times* – a form of message branding (Castells 2009: 419) – makes it only more effective in its subsequent construction work. This background made its deployment by those opposing the concept of anthropogenic global warming, most notably conservative bloggers, opinion writers and pundits, a relatively simple task, if only initially. As 'knowledge', it was then contested – Dykstra did so by simply revealing its history – limiting to some degree its capacity to challenge social concerns about the risk of climate change. The dynamics at work here are complex. Meanings, strategies, histories, ideologies, journalistic practices, competition; all are at play. The result is mediated knowledge, a mediated version of reality.

News constructs a reality separate from actual reality – but how separate? The degree of separation remains hotly debated. Alison Anderson, in her analysis of the 1990s UK controversies over the disposal of the oil rig Brent Spar and dying seals, takes issue with 'extreme forms of social constructionism which assert that we cannot make any assumptions about an objective "reality".' This, she argues, suggests that 'one account of reality is of no more intrinsic value than another' (1997: 13).

Most of us would concede that there are few problems in establishing the objective 'reality' of a tree or a tiger unless we wish to question every assumption we make in the course of everyday life. However, making judgements about the reality of, say, global warming is clearly much more complex since there are many contending viewpoints and vested interests involved. Moreover, journalistic accounts are inevitably selective since they are influenced by, among other things, news values, news formats, editorial and advertising pressures, news sources and personal commitments. Also much reporting of environmental affairs involves simplifying complex scientific and technical information. (Anderson 1997: 14)

Viewing news as socially and culturally constructed, the product of a complex array of often historically located meanings, practices and ideas, allows researchers to engage in news as a contested site, where 'truth' and 'reality' as presented in the news are open for negotiation in the news-making process. Boundaries do exist around these negotiations, but they are also constructed via shared cultural and social understandings. Likewise, we can begin to see news media as involved in an equally complex process of meaning making, constructing ideas and social norms – and sometimes challenging them.

But how do news texts do their work? How do they contribute to the body of understandings that constitute our social and cultural conditions, that influence our personal and political decision making, that impact on ourselves and our environments? To return briefly to the contested component of the *New York Times* story on polar bears: 'Other experts see a healthier population. They note that there are more than 20,000 polar bears roaming the Arctic, compared to as few as 5,000 40 years ago . . .'. Now consider the following discourse features: First, although not sourced to a specific scientist, the use of the term 'other experts' compensates somewhat by serving in its numerical vagueness in the sentence to suggest, if not the existence of scientific consensus, at least a scientific balance. Second, 'see', in this context, also serves a legitimating role; while not a scientifically precise verb, such as 'record', 'prove' or 'identify', it works through its connection with the subject of the sentence, 'other experts', to suggest direct observation of the 'healthier population'. Third, the use of figures works to provide the 'fact' with credibility with the precision of '40 years' compensating a little for the vague nature of 'as few as 5,000'. So even in this small example, we can see a news text at work, potentially creating understandings, opening spaces for contestation and discouraging others, and doing this simply through word choice and sentence structure (for discussions of news discourse and approaches, see Bell 1991, 1998; Fowler 1991; van Dijk 1991).

Within media and journalism studies, there are numerous ways of analysing news texts. A fuller analysis of the *New York Times* story, for example, might also consider media 'frames' (see especially Gitlin 1980; Entman 1993; and below); quantitative elements, for example, how many times the word 'experts' is used throughout the story (Hansen et al. 1998); layout, accompanying images or headlines (Rose 2001; Deacon at al. 2007); which sources are quoted and how; and overall political, social and ideological contexts (Fairclough 1998). Here, similar terms may be deployed to describe subtly or sometimes greatly varying methods. Confusion over terms such as 'frame' or 'discourse' or 'content' analysis can unnecessarily hinder those seeking to understand how news texts work, more so for those seeking – as this book does – to synthesize analyses from various research traditions and disciplines (see Entman 1993; Garrett and Bell 1998: 2; Deacon et al. 2007). A detailed discussion of the many methods in use is beyond the scope of this book. However, here it is useful to make two brief points. The first point is that as news itself operates across many levels (personal, professional, organizational, institutional, and across time and space) and is influenced by diverse and complex factors (economic, political, historical, cultural), we need a wide range of interconnected methods and ways of understanding news if we are able to untangle even small parts of the web. Barbie Zelizer, for example, calls for the development of scholarly frameworks that can accommodate journalism's 'vagaries, downsides, and inconsistencies as easily as they address the more coherent dimensions of the journalistic world', a way of thinking about journalism and its study 'through a necessarily interdisciplinary lens' (2004: 213). A second related point is that both text and context are important for the study of news. While the balance between these will vary from method to method – a frame analysis, for example, will be more concerned with text while a critical discourse analysis aims to integrate text more fully with context (Carvalho 2007: 227) – it is essential to recognize that no texts work alone. Boundaries are often needed to define and manage research, but that does not make these boundaries any firmer than, for example, a journalist's decision to focus on only one event or angle of a large and complex issue in a story. Overall, as more connections can be made between various approaches, the more will be revealed about media roles and responsibilities in environmental debate.

The emergence of climate change as a globally recognized risk and thus topic for news media has necessarily seen the emergence of such studies. Anabela Carvalho's work, deploying methods adapted from critical discourse analysis, has revealed a number of important features about climate change news in the UK, and its changing relationship over several decades to science and under-lying political currents. For example, in the quality broadsheet coverage up to 1988, scientists were the 'uncontested central actors and exclusive definers' of climate change (2007: 228). This was achieved in, among other ways, by sourcing articles to the influential scientific journals *Nature* and *Science* and by naming researchers and their institutional affiliation. However, this changed at the end of 1988 with then Prime Minister Margaret Thatcher's appropriation of the risks of climate change to support a case for nuclear energy over coal and thus to weaken the coal industry. At the end of 1988, according to Carvalho, 'the scope of potentially necessary political, social and economic trans-formations to address climate change started to become visible' (2007: 229), while previously climate change was represented as a potentially solvable scientific problem.

This politicization combined with scientific uncertainty, creating a space for ideological interpretations within media coverage. Initial coverage of the First Assessment Report of the Intergovernmental Panel on Climate Change (IPCC) in the conservative newspaper *The Times*, for example, followed Thatcher's proposition, but as climate change focus heightened, became increasingly reactionary. For the *Sunday Times* in 1990, scientists were 'deeply divided about how much global warming will result from an increase in greenhouse gases', and elsewhere expressed fear that 'in a fit of excessive and emotional environmentalism, governments could squander billions that might be better spent elsewhere' (quoted in Carvalho 2007: 230). Carvalho writes that by 1990, 'Governmental moves to control and recontextualize understandings of the greenhouse effect led to most media discourse being taken over by politicians and other actors' (2007: 231). Science had lost most of its initial 'high ground in definitions'.

The Second Assessment Report from the IPCC was released five years later, and this time clearly connected human activities with climate change and advocated substantial measures to mitigate against human impact. Yet, while the science was becoming more solid and consensual, an 'image of uncertainty and disagreement was amplified by *The Times* and by some in the *Independent*' (Carvalho 2007: 232). American 'sceptics' were given space in *The Times*, despite their known connections to fossil fuel companies or conservative political organizations, while coverage in the *Independent* depended in part on who wrote the article. Meanwhile, the *Guardian* constructed, in several articles from this period but not consistently, a sense of crisis and urgency (Carvalho 2007: 234–5). By 2001, *The Times* had become less concerned with challenging science as scientific evidence became clearly weighted towards consensus. Nevertheless, it dedicated only one article to the IPCC report in early 2001, as opposed to the four published by the *Independent* and three by the *Guardian*. Overall, Carvalho's analysis finds a clear connection to ideology in the journalism produced about climate change, not only in opinion articles but also in news items. She concludes:

> Firstly, ideology has implications for the interpretation of *'facts'*. The reliability attributed by the media to scientific 'truth' claims, the preferred definitions of 'facts,' and the quantity of media space

dedicated to a given scientific claim simultaneously derive from and sustain a certain ideology. Secondly, the recognized *agents* of definition of scientific knowledge vary as a function of ideological standings. The selection of 'experts' and 'counter-experts' that are given voice depends on and reproduces certain worldviews. Thirdly, the goals associated with knowledge also have an ideological basis. The direct or indirect implications for individual or governmental action that are drawn from scientific claims result from views of the status quo and contribute to consolidating or challenging it. (Carvalho 2007: 237, original emphasis)

Here, then, newspapers are clearly working to construct an understanding, a 'knowledge', about science and climate change. Carvalho proposes a political reading of science reports in the press because just as the media clearly 'read scientific papers politically, so should we read the newspapers'. In this way, audiences could engage in a 'more active interpretation of representations of knowledge in the media and in a critical understanding of their implications' (2007: 240). Engagement is something to which we will return in Chapter Seven. In the meantime, focus remains on the producers of news, and in particular the norms and values of their professional practices.

Making news

Journalists are driven by many factors in their daily work. Stories need to meet a range of criteria concerning, for example, news values, structure and presentation, and source credibility for reporters to be seen by colleagues, employers and news consumers as doing their job. Professional discourses about 'objectivity', 'fourth estate' and 'independence' also play a part, as do personal ambitions, preferences, ideologies and relationships. Two other factors commonly identified as determining how a journalist will go about his or her daily work are time and space (see Tuchman 1978). A newspaper or news bulletin must be produced to a certain length at a regular time. The concept of deadlines may have been altered with the growth in web-based and other round-the-clock news services but it nevertheless survives as a powerful determiner, particularly when combined with the growing demand for 'immediacy' (see Flew 2008; also Allan 2006). Individual journalists are required to file space-filling stories regularly. That is a primary role as defined by their employers. This is not to say that other factors are unimportant, only that they will be embedded within the time and space constraints. For example, a journalist will seek out stories that meet widely accepted criteria for newsworthiness, thereby minimizing the need for editorial discussion and negotiation, and sources who can provide material, hopefully in usable form, within a certain time period. This section will consider some of the practices, values and expectations that contribute to determining what news we read about the environment.

Newspapers, playwright George Bernard Shaw once said, are seemingly unable to discriminate between a bicycle accident and the collapse of civilization (quoted in Franklin et al. 2005: 163). It is an insightful comment on the slippery nature of news values. When placed beside the journalist's comment which began this chapter – editors wanting water lapping at the doors of readers before being convinced of the value of climate change stories – and some of the factors already noted in this and previous chapters that contribute to the openness of news and the movement of issues in and through the media arena and public sphere, the complexity and contingent nature of the processes at work begin to emerge. The journalistic values that influence the content and presentation of news texts are rarely articulated in any depth in newsrooms: journalists just 'know' a good story when they 'see' one. This is not to say that a story's overall value or even its individual elements are not discussed and debated within newsrooms. It may have a local or celebrity element or good pictures or quotes that make it more worthy of a place in the news mix of the day. The news mix itself is also important, and any newsroom debate about a story's overall value will be held in the context of not only what stories are available to that particular outlet but also potentially to its competitors. However, journalists rarely consider generally or theorize the elements that make a 'good' story and the values they use in a story's production, selection of content and determination of worth. This suggests a hegemonic, unquestioning acceptance of the structures of news work. But this is too simple an explanation.

An early but still influential attempt to theorize news values by analysing news texts comes from Johan Galtung and Mari Holmboe Ruge, who studied Norwegian newspaper coverage of three foreign events (1965). Their central question was: how do 'events' become 'news'? As environmental risks often become news via an event, such as a disaster or protest (Molotch and Lester 1975; Miller and Riechert 2000: 51), environmental news coverage is commonly studied through a lens focused on news values as they appear in news texts. For Galtung and Ruge, events need to satisfy the conditions of the following factors to be newsworthy:

1. *Frequency*. This refers to how long it takes for an event to unfold and take on meaning. An event is more likely to become news if this time span is similar to the rhythms and frequency of news.
2. *Threshold*. The bigger an event, the more likely it is to be recorded, and a threshold exists that the event has to pass before it is recorded at all.
3. *Unambiguity*. The less ambiguity the more the event will be noticed. News does not necessarily prefer simple events, but it does prefer events with clear interpretations.
4. *Meaningfulness*. Making meaning is easier when the event can be interpreted within the cultural framework of the news audience, that is, where cultural proximity exists. But relevant events may also happen in far off places if they are filled with meaning for the audience.
5. *Consonance*. How much a person predicts or wants an event to happen affects his or her capacity to register it. Accordingly, if an event is too far away from the expectation, it will not be registered.
6. *Unexpectedness*. Providing some correction to the previous two points, events that are regular and institutionalized, continuing and repetitive, will not attract much attention. Those that are unexpected or rare, but also meaningful and consonant, will become news.

7. *Continuity*. Once defined as news, it is more likely to stay in the news, even when its connection to other news values declines.
8. *Composition*. If a news bulletin is dominated by foreign news, it will be harder for a foreign news event to become news. This refers to the news mix, noted earlier.

Applying this framework, it is possible to glimpse why some stories emerge into the media arena, and others do not. Climate change, for example, struggles on a number of fronts: it rarely meets the demands of the 24-hour news cycle in that it has no immediate resolution (water is only rarely lapping at the doors of readers) and it contains a great deal of ambiguity. Debate also largely takes place within institutionalized routines, making it unattractive for editors. However, during 2005 and 2006, a number of events transpired that met Galtung and Ruge's criteria and climate change became news. Notable among these was Hurricane Katrina, which devastated parts of the US Gulf, including New Orleans, in 2005. This was a large unambiguous event, to which news audiences around the world could relate. The severity of the weather event served to piggyback climate change into the news. Once there, and supported by a number of related events, it stayed as news in its own right.

According to Galtung and Ruge, these factors are devised by considering 'what facilitates and what impedes perception' and are therefore culture-free in the sense they are not expected to vary significantly from one culture to another. However, they list a second set of factors that influence the transition of events to news, ones that are culture-bound. In Scandinavia, they identified:

1. *Elite nations*. An event connected to an elite nation is more likely to become news.
2. *Elite people*. Likewise, for elite people. In both cases, such events are likely to have greater consequences than those that concern non-elite nations and people. But elites can also serve to stand for everybody, as followers of celebrity news know.
3. *Personification*. An event seen in personal terms and caused by

the action of specific individuals is more likely to become news. This is a more complex process, in part connected to news' demand for a subject, active verb and object in every sentence (that is, a perpetrator, 'crime' and a victim), and news images of people rather than just landscapes and buildings.

4. *Negativity*. It is easier to report bad news than good. Negative news, the authors argue, meets many of the other criteria noted above more easily than positive news: in frequency (bad events tend to unfold completely between two newspaper issues); consensus and unambiguity (there tends to be more agreement that the event is, indeed, bad); consonance (we expect bad things to happen); and unexpectedness (positive events tend to unfold in a regular flow).

The impact of Hurricane Katrina on the elite United States and the intervention of former US Vice President Al Gore through his film *An Inconvenient Truth* worked to push climate change onto the news agenda in countries around the world, illustrating the applicability of Galtung and Ruge's culturally specific values. Nevertheless, it is important to also stress that significant variations do occur not only between countries and the media systems to which they ascribe (Hallin and Mancini 2004) but also between media within national boundaries. Television, radio, newspapers and online information will vary in their application of news criteria – the need for personification through radio, for example, presents a different set of demands than the need for visual images of people for much television current affairs programming – while there will also be significant differences between regional and national media, community and commercial radio, broadsheet and tabloid newspapers, even within newsrooms between various news 'sections' and journalistic roles. The application of journalistic values is highly context dependent. Likewise, such schema as Galtung and Ruge's cannot get at behind-the-scenes discussions or practices by sources or journalists, nor reflect the full complexity of journalistic decision making and values. They do, however, highlight the fact that news making is a professional practice with its own values, and can begin the work of explaining how some events become news rather than others, if not complete it alone.

In a variation to the concept of news values, Maxwell Boykoff and Jules Boykoff use the term 'journalistic norms' to analyse US media coverage of climate change coverage from 1988–2004, illustrating how vulnerable climate change as an issue has been to factors that influence news practice (2007; see also Boykoff and Boykoff 2004). Personalization, dramatization and novelty are dubbed first-order journalistic norms, 'significant and baseline influences on both the selection of what is news and the content of news stories' (2007: 1192). Authority-order, where journalists seek out authoritative sources, and balance, where opposing views are provided with equal space, are described as second-order journalistic norms, 'initiated and informed' by the three previous norms. For Boykoff and Boykoff, 'Real-world issues, events and dynamics must interact with journalistic norms in order to successfully translate into media coverage' (2007: 1195). Anthropogenic climate change and other environmental issues may climb to the top of the media agenda not for scientific reasons or 'alarmed discovery' (Downs 1972) but because of their interaction with these norms. Drawing on a sample of almost 5,000 stories from influential newspapers and television news bulletins, the authors found that there had been notable increases in global warming coverage in 1988, 1990, 1992, 1997, 2001–2 and 2004. In 1988, for example, the novelty of a weather scare (drought), combined with dramatic statements from UK Prime Minister Margaret Thatcher and US President George Bush (climate change was 'serious'), with the personalization of a well-known and respected scientist James Hansen (who testified that it was ninety-nine per cent certain that global warming had begun), 'meant that this story conformed to the journalistic norms and informational predilections of the newspaper and television news media' (Boykoff and Boykoff 2007: 1196). Science, the authors claim, was not the dominant influence. The same was true for the 1990 and 1992 peaks. However, the personalization of the coverage drew attention away from the underlying causes of the problem, 'favouring the strategic moves of individuals over the political contexts in which they operate' (2007: 1197). For example, would Bush attend the Rio de Janeiro Earth Summit (the United Nations Conference on Environment and Development in Brazil) or not? Similarly, first-order norms were invoked in 2001–2 when newly elected George W. Bush took an unequivocal stance against the Kyoto Protocol – all 'sheer novelty and authority'.

And what of the in-between times, the 'slow years of climate change coverage'? Here, according to Boykoff and Boykoff, while important events and debate occurred about climate change, it did not translate into a form that so easily met first-order journalistic norms and therefore received less in-depth coverage. What emerged instead was the balancing of duelling scientists. 'While international conferences, new scientific reports, and political promises might fuse into an amorphous swirl of cautious language that is unable to meet journalistic demands for freshness and novelty, the ever present duelling scientist could be relied upon for a dramatic dose of disagreement,' the authors write (2007: 1200). This served to distort unfolding science and policy discourse and to breed confusion within the general public about the difference between widely accepted knowledge and 'highly speculative claims' (2007: 1200). Nevertheless, without this 'controversy', it is likely that there would have been even less coverage during these periods.

Overall, the authors conclude that climate change coverage is inextricably connected to journalistic norms, and as media coverage of climate change matters, so too is it important to understand how such norms operate:

> The rhythms and rituals of journalism do not simply cohere into a static structural factor; rather, they are built and buttressed by the everyday practitioners of journalism: reporters and editors who are enmeshed in political and professional discourses and normative orders. Therefore, journalistic norms not only interlock into important structures but they also embed themselves in the minds of journalists operating within these structures of interaction. Since these norms are formed collectively, they are not eradicated from the minds of journalism workers without great difficulty, in part because, as with many social customs and routines, global-warming news production has many tacit facets and unarticulated assumptions. Thus, by employing

the norms of professional journalism, the mass media can adversely affect interactions between science, policy and the public. (Boykoff and Boykoff 2007: 1201)

But are news producers simply unknowing slaves to the values, norms and routines influencing their profession? While editors may have had great difficulty with climate change as an issue prior to its emergence as a widely acknowledged global crisis, journalists have for some time found ways to ensure its coverage, in part by co-opting and manipulating these very news values and journalistic narrative devices. For example, as Joe Smith found, they may use located stories on flood damage, coastal erosion or the arrival of an exotic disease or species to 'give editors a place on a map with a name, a dramatic image – almost a personality – and a clearly figured denouement such as "when will it fall into the sea"' (Smith 2005: 1477). This works to both subvert journalistic values and norms – that is, strategically deploying values and norms to widen coverage beyond usually acceptable stories – and to further entrench them, by ensuring stories still fit the criteria they set.

A useful concept to consider here is frames, which can help provide a more nuanced explanation of the activities of news producers than an analysis of values or norms alone. Todd Gitlin provides an influential definition in his study of media and the US student movement:

> *Media* frames, largely unspoken and unacknowledged, organize the world both for journalists who report it and, in some important degree, for us who rely on their reports. *Media frames are persistent patterns of cognition, interpretation, and presentation, of selection, emphasis, and exclusion, by which symbol-handlers routinely organize discourse, whether verbal or visual.* Frames enable journalists to process large amounts of information quickly and routinely: to recognize it as information, to assign it to cognitive categories, and to package it for efficient relay to their audiences. Thus, for organizational reasons alone, frames are unavoidable, and journalism is organized to regulate their production. (Gitlin 1980: 7, original emphasis)

Frames can define problems, diagnose causes, make moral judgements and suggest remedies (Entman 1993: 52). They work by highlighting some pieces of information – 'elevating them in salience' – which means that they make them 'more noticeable, meaningful, or memorable to audiences' (Entman 1993: 53). Once this has occurred, audiences are more likely to recognize, process and remember the information, which will in turn contribute to the continued use of the frame by journalists to ensure their own credibility and the understanding of their audience. Frames are thus further sites of deep contestation: 'the frame in a news text is really the imprint of power – it registers the identity of actors or interests that competed to dominate the text' (Entman 1993: 55).

However, just as journalists can exploit their norms and values to cover stories that editors would not normally be interested in, they can also co-opt dominant frames, as Smith found in working group discussions with journalists. They described using the UK floods of 2000 to cover climate change by bringing their stories within acceptable news frames such as government competence, security of homes and insurance risks, and vulnerable social groups (Smith 2005: 1477). Yet, as Smith points out, the negotiation between editors and journalists is a critical point in relation to climate change coverage, and generally takes place within the context of immense time pressures, as well as hierarchical scrutiny of the editor's performance. This often leads to decisions to take a journalistic conservative approach based largely on what competitors are likely to be covering that day. 'The result is very likely to be stories that satisfy editorial standards much more satisfactorily than they communicate the social or scientific reality or significance of an issue as understood by specialists,' Smith writes (2005: 1477).

What these examples do is hint at the existence of much deeper layers of complexity and contingency underlying news production, layers that text-based analyses of values and norms are not readily able to uncover. The practices of news making, the strategic activities of sources, the symbolism that flows in and around news and the active involvement of news audiences clearly point to the fact that journalism does not exist in an impenetrable bubble, but rather within a complex web of interactions, meaning making and power relations, many of which can only be revealed via 'behind-the-scenes' studies of journalistic and source activity.

Nevertheless, structures formed by news values, narratives and deadlines, as well as newsroom hierarchies and professional and financial competition, obviously impact greatly on the content of news. While some journalists adopt such values and work within professional boundaries unquestioningly, others deploy them to expand what would otherwise be an even more limited coverage. And just as it is a mistake to see news values and norms as uniform across national and regional boundaries and from outlet to outlet, so too would it be a mistake to see them as set across the different styles of journalism, sometimes practised within single newsrooms. An investigative journalist or one specifically assigned the environmental 'round' or 'beat' may interpret and be guided differently by professional practices than a 'general' journalist, for example. As technological and economic changes impact news, these interpretations will also shift across time. As such, the next section considers how recent changes to news production and culture are impacting on media coverage of environmental issues, and does so by focusing on continuing journalistic anxieties around the concepts of objectivity and advocacy.

Changing news

Throughout its history, environmental journalism has attempted to balance a role of scrutinizing the activities, policies and impacts of industry and government – the generators of environmental policy, policing and harm – with an ideological position that the environment and the politics that surround it do matter. Here its aims become closely aligned with those of the environment movement. This leaves environmental journalism, when practised as a distinct 'round' or 'beat' within mainstream newsrooms or as an investigative practice focused on environmental conflicts, vulnerable to accusations of advocacy, of lacking objectivity and of bias. While advocacy journalism may be to many a positive practice that leads to social change, only a fine line separates it from accusations of bias. Such anxieties are found not only in the well resourced and powerful counter-claims of government and industry, but in the professional journalistic values and norms around the concept of objectivity. However, if environmental journalism foregoes an investigative role to concentrate on science, long-term trends or nature writing, it loses newsworthiness, an obvious 'news peg', and a place within the news. The environment round or beat is often the first to go when news organizations suffer financial cuts, and reconstituted only when the environment re-emerges strongly onto the social and political agenda (Dawson 2009–10: 20). We might ask whether its often uncomfortable fit within the newsroom and thus its vulnerability is founded in part on its distinct relationship with the concept of journalistic objectivity, and an historical overview that also considers recent economic, technological and professional shifts helps provide an answer.

Objectivity is a key tenet in news culture, central to the discourses that circulate within and around journalism (Tuchman 1972, 1978; Gans 1979). To be objective is to be 'factual', 'unbiased'. It is also, as Gaye Tuchman showed in the 1970s, a 'strategic ritual' designed to protect daily journalism from the risks associated with 'deadlines, libel suits, and superiors' demands' (1972: 661). As such, it helps structure how journalists go about their daily work, the sources they turn to and how they present facts. However, just as 'facts' need to be read as constructed knowledge, so too does the relationship between journalism and objectivity. It is a relationship rooted in historical change, change prompted by economic, technological, political and social shifts, and change in how journalism does things, what it believes, what it means, and importantly, what makes it special.

Few early nineteenth-century newspapers had qualms about taking a firm and often aggressive position on public issues, including the environment, as shown in Chapter One. Before the revolution of the mass market 'pauper' and 'penny' presses in the UK and US in the first half of the century, newspapers were in the main communicating with an elite audience. While writers had called upon ideas of fairness and non-partisanship since the earliest days of the press, it was not until the market changes of the nineteenth century that explicit notions of objectivity became integrated into the newly professionalized activity and identity of journalism (Tuchman 1978: 160–1; Neuzil 2008: 131). Economics partly drove the change, with newspapers that took a radical, strongly partisan or oppositional stance finding their potential markets too narrow to survive in the emerging commercial environment. The new breed of newspapers also perceived a demand from their readers for a focus on the everyday, on the events that impacted on their lives, and for 'facts' (Allan 2004: 15). The spread of the electric telegraph in the 1840s produced an emphasis among journalists on daily-ness – 'one which promoted a peculiar fascination for facts devoid of "appreciation" to communicate a sense of an instantaneous present' (Allan 2004: 16). The late nineteenth century saw journalists become increasingly professionalized, and by the end of the First World War and a growing awareness of the potential of state and industry propaganda campaigns, objectivity had become a central and, indeed, institutionalized value (Allan 2004: 23). Research, investigation, fairness; these terms came to coexist with objectivity in the lexicon deployed by journalists to describe themselves and their practices.

Nevertheless, the 'campaign' survived, if compartmentalized and limited within and by the commercial concerns of these new types of publications, and continues to exist in contemporary newspapers and news programming. One genre of campaign that survives allows the presence of radical voices within an otherwise journalistically conservative coverage. These voices are generally clearly identified as separate from the news organization's normal work and therefore restricted in their meaning and potential reach (Conboy 2004: 108). George Monbiot's weekly column in the UK's *Guardian* newspaper is an example of this. While Monbiot might describe owners of weekenders as Britain's most selfish people, it is not a position advocated elsewhere in the newspaper (Monbiot 2008: 152–6). A second type of campaign may merge various components of a media organization's roles – including news and opinion/editorials – to openly push for change. In the 1980s, for example, the *Age* newspaper in Australia ran a campaign to clean up the Yarra River, which flows through the newspaper's circulation area of Melbourne and surrounds. It used investigative reporters, news and feature writers, photographers and opinion and editorial columns to produce a series that insisted on government action. Each item ran with the badging, 'Give the Yarra a Go', and thus the newspaper could remain immune to the charge of bias. This, after all, was clearly identified as separate from the actual journalism, the real work, of the newspaper. Moreover, responsibility for the river pollution was located both historically and amongst many. No-one in particular was to blame.

A third type of 'campaign' is perhaps the most troubling for mainstream journalism: here, the journalistic tenets of research and investigation are deployed to focus on a specific area that the journalist – and possibly his or her media outlet – clearly sees in need of change. Often, there is an identifiable perpetrator, someone to blame. While certainly not limited to news about the environment, it is a style of journalism closely associated with specialized reporting on the environment. When, for example, journalists chose to investigate and reveal the harmful effects of pesticides produced by Danish chemical company Cheminova on developing countries, investigative journalism became a 'political act within the boundaries of professional journalistic standards', activist-like in its critical framing of the issues (Olesen 2008: 247, 261). According to Mark Neuzil, environmental journalism was dominated by such 'campaigns' throughout the twentieth century, and even the adoption of the environment as a specific beat within mainstream newsrooms in the 1960s and 1970s did not dispel the association with advocacy. These journalists 'transformed stories about the environment from ones driven by dramatic events and government leaks to something more investigative, crusading, in-depth, and in many cases full-time' (Neuzil 2008: 186).

Why, when the 'best' and most awarded journalism is that which prompts policy or social change, is the concept of 'crusading' or 'advocacy' journalism an uncomfortable one within the profession? As Tuchman pointed out in 1978, crusades have a clear place within mainstream journalism but that place is bounded by professional norms and practices:

> Not only must newsworkers be factual, but facts must also be fair. By balancing opinions of newsmakers and weighing evidence,

newsworkers must strive to achieve a fair presentation of the facts in order both to inform the public and to maintain credibility. They may launch crusades, as did the journalists of the 1890s, but they must do so in a spirit of fairness that aims to protect the public from the excesses of government, and the government from the excesses of people. (Tuchman 1978: 161)

In part, discomfiture with this type of 'crusade' may result from the alignment of the goals of environmental or investigative journalism with those of the environment movement, and the conflict this creates between more powerful and 'legitimate' institutional sources, such as government and big business. As Olesen points out, the Danish documentaries, focusing only on the negative effects of pesticides, failed to discuss their benefits to developing countries (2008: 261). This may only be a problem, however, if counter-arguments are drowned out in subsequent public debate (Olesen 2008: 261). Of course, we also need to take into account changing newsroom practices and logics, particularly those that have seen less resources put towards investigative and/or environmental journalism in recent times, while – as will be discussed in the next chapter – more resources are provided towards ensuring counter-arguments or only selected information reach the public for debate.

Environmental journalism, particularly in the United States where it emerged from a tradition of nature writing, has blurred many of the lines mainstream journalism uses to define itself. Here, a more overt connection exists to activism in a number of forms. From a news practice perspective, this passage hints at how boundaries between 'objective' reporting and advocacy journalism have come to be permeated:

The late 1980s and early 1990s were salad days for the environmental beat in the United States. *Time* magazine, departing from its tradition of picking a human, selected the Earth as 'Planet of the Year' for 1988. Publications that had previously ignored environmental coverage, such as *Business Week*, devoted staff to the topic; the *Rocky Mountain News* and other newspapers added a daily page for environment and science stories; local television stations created environmental teams; and PBS ran a ten-part series called *Race to Save the Planet* in fall 1990. Organizers of the twentieth anniversary of Earth Day in 1990 took full advantage of the increased media attention to get their message out. (Neuzil 2008: 196)

How does 'journalism' labelled *Race to Save the Planet* or opening journalism to be taken 'advantage' of by sources with an environmental agenda fit the commonly accepted professional concept of objectivity? This blurring, combined with the popularity of the campaign as a genre in environmental journalism, has undoubtedly contributed to anxiety about and marginalization of the area within mainstream media organizations.

Unsurprisingly, the questions of objectivity and advocacy are far from straightforward for journalists themselves who cover the environment. In 2006, five top US environmental reporters were asked about objectivity (Neuzil 2008: 231). Four of the five said they were uncomfortable in an advocacy role, but all five said they avoided the 'he said, she said' type of stories as a way of balancing conflicting opinions and 'facts'. The science should speak for itself. Activism, said one respondent, was evident only in the subjects he chose to write about. According to Andrew Revkin, of the *New York Times*: 'There is something of a false dichotomy in the notion that being an objective reporter is at odds with being a "concerned citizen". Of course I'm concerned about the quality of the environment' (quoted in Neuzil 2008: 231–2). However, retired *Boston Globe* reporter Ross Gelbspan described his shift from reporter to 'advocate to semi-activist' once he began covering climate change, 'although it's critically important to me not to say or write anything of substance that I have not documented or verified' (quoted in Neuzil 2008: 232).

Such debates are likely to become louder in the face of the internet's rise, and its insistence through 'news' websites and blogs that we rethink what we mean by objectivity and journalism itself? Attempts to categorize and catalogue 'journalism' on the internet are still risky. The rate and range of change mean that new forms and styles are emerging simultaneously, as are new ways of doing 'journalism'. Wikis, Twitter, Facebook all have at times promoted at the very least subtle shifts in how we think about journalism as a practice and its relationship with its sources and audiences (see Allan 2006). Participatory and citizen journalisms, increased audience interactivity, blogs by journalists and blogs about journalism are among the many new forms that are emerging. When viewed alongside an increasingly globalized setting for the production of news, we can expect profound challenges to our understanding of what constitutes journalism and the professional values that underpin it.

Brian McNair usefully identifies four broad categories of online actor connected to the production of 'journalism': *professional-institutional actors*, including websites of transnational satellite broadcasters, newspapers and national broadcasters, and of internet-only journalistic organizations, such as *Slate*; *professional-individual actors*, or journalists that write for their own websites; *non-professional-institutional actors*, including government agencies, NGOs, political parties, campaigning and lobby groups, and terrorist organizations; and *non-professional-individual actors*, or private bloggers, numbering in their millions (2006: 199). According to McNair, early forms of online journalism, such as *Slate* or the gossip column *Drudge Report*, quickly established a fundamental distinction in the evolution of online news media, 'that between established professionalism and iconoclastic amateurism':

> Or, to put it another way, the distinction between, on the one hand, journalism aspiring to the ethics and standards espoused by print and broadcast news media for centuries and, on the other, journalism (though many disputed that it could be described as such) founded on alternative principles having less to do with the values of objectivity and reliability than with subjectivity, immediacy, and independence from, even rejection of, established journalistic institutions. (McNair 2006: 119)

For Stuart Allan, an 'us vs them cycle' has been playing out between mainstream journalists and bloggers, with objectivity a focus of the debate. And here the constructed nature of journalistic 'objectivity' comes to the fore:

Few would deny that blogs are inherently subjective, in line with their authors' perspectives or predispositions; indeed, for many bloggers, a non-biased blog would be pointless, even if it was possible to achieve. Accordingly, the usually tacit, unspoken rules of mainstream reporting will more likely than not be rendered problematic by bloggers providing alternative accounts, facts or interpretations. That is to say, the 'objective' reporter's decisions about how best to write a particular story – everything from judging which source is credible to which adjective seems appropriate – will be recognized as being 'subjective' to the extent that they are rendered transparent via the bloggers' scrutiny. (Allan 2006: 85)

Nor should the contribution from readers as fact checkers and their collective knowledge be underestimated in the online world. 'What counts as objectivity, it follows, necessarily takes on a more nuanced inflection as differing viewpoints multiply accordingly,' writes Allan (2006: 85). Popular US environmental blogger, David Roberts of *Gristmill*, puts it succinctly, while comparing bloggers to the pamphleteers of early American journalism: 'Having thousands of readers bird-dogging you keeps you pretty honest' (quoted in Neuzil 2008: 229).

With its often uncomfortable fit within mainstream news agendas and newsrooms, environmental journalism quickly appeared in various forms on the internet. Former mainstream journalists eager to make available more in-depth coverage of environmental issues established some sites as news wire services. Others grew out of NGOs. Environmental Health Services, a not-for-profit organization working to 'increase public understanding of environmental exposures and human health', established *Environmental Health News*, for example (Neuzil 2008: 228). *Grist*, a now independent website read by half a million people a month in 2006, began as a project of Earth Day Network.

Thousands of blogs on environmental issues have emerged in the United States alone, and some by mainstream journalists. While news journalists were initially often discouraged from blogging by their employers because of perceived conflicts of interest or as undermining journalistic values (Allan 2006: 86), it is now common practice. In the US, veteran environmental reporters from the *Seattle Post-Intelligence*, Lisa Stiffler and Robert McLure, established *Dateline Earth*, because, 'we wanted really to be able to write about the stuff that was falling through the cracks, whether it was something quirky and local or something national or international that was beyond the scope of what the P-I's usual coverage includes,' Stiffler said (quoted in Neuzil 2008: 230). Nevertheless, bloggers and journalists continue the debate over practice, summed up here by environmental blogger, Alex Steffen of *Worldchanging*: 'Journalists are obliged to give somebody who is doing something awful, or who holds a distinctly minority opinion, a voice equal to that of those who are trying to alert people to a problem purely out of public interest' (quoted in Neuzil 2008: 229).

Like objectivity, 'public interest' is a term that dominates journalism's own internal discourse and the discourses of those who monitor its activities and practices. In the quote above, it is seconded by journalism's primary competitor to further its claims to credibility; that blogs are better able to circulate information produced 'purely out of public interest'. It is too early to know where such bids will leave journalism's own claims to significance, its professional practices and identities, and its anxieties. Never immune to change, the values and routines that structure the production of news will undoubtedly shift to accommodate new competitors, technologies and pressures. There will be emerging opportunities for the widespread communication of information about the environment; other important doors will close. The quote above also usefully emphasizes the importance of sources in the construction of journalistic identity and practice. This book argues that once we look beyond news texts to the practices behind their production, deeper layers of complexities and contradictions emerge. This becomes even clearer in the next chapter, which focuses on the multiple sources and voices of environmental news, and the dynamics driving their representation and influence in public debate.

4

Sources and Voices

One of the mothers, Kesar Bhai, held her 12-year-old son Suraj in her arms. She had inhaled the noxious fumes in 1984 and was hospitalized but recovered. Her son, Suraj, was born brain damaged and cannot sit or talk. 'My husband is a labourer. We have no money to spend on our son. He cannot even eat on his own. I get free medical care for my breathing difficulties because I am a gas victim. My child does not get any help but he has been affected.' (2008 report in the *Guardian*, UK, on the legacy of the Bhopal toxic gas leak in India, from American multinational Union Carbide's pesticide plant, in which 3000 people died in one night)

Who are the voices of the environment? Who are the sources of information? Who is allowed to speak? And how? Journalists, the oft repeated aphorism goes, are only as good as their sources. Even for this reason alone, they are inclined to keep these sources, and the contact book or database in which their sources' details are kept, close to their chests. But it is not just the contacts' names, phone numbers or email addresses that are protected. More hidden are the details of the relationship between sources and journalists, the ways in which sources and voices are used by and use journalists, how information is located and ranked on the basis of its providers, the negotiations and struggles that take place over news access and, ultimately, the representation of sources themselves. Michael Schudson calls sources 'the deep, dark secret of the power of the press' (2003: 134), a description that can be extended to all forms of news media. As argued in previous chapters, news is a valued space, evidenced by the level of contestation that takes place over access, in terms of both entry to the news arena, or coverage, but more importantly over attaining continuing positive access and to the benefits, the power, that only this kind of access can provide. So great are the potential rewards that sources not only continue to develop strategies and commit major resources to media relations but will, in fact, become symbiotically connected to the media, restructured and attuned towards the aim of entering the media arena. Undoubtedly, the stakes are high for sources, but they are in fact much higher in a broader sense, for here are located many anxieties about news media roles and responsibilities in contemporary democratic debate.

Within mediated environmental politics, these are the voices of scientists, politicians, industry representatives, public relations consultants, environmental activists, and ordinary people concerned or affected by environmental change and risk. My aim in this chapter is to identify the actions and routine practices that influence when and how these voices are heard within and through media, many of which have evolved and continue to evolve to achieve media access. Primary features of the relationships between news media and their sources, and between and within sources, will also be identified. These relationships are highly reflexive: awareness of one's own practices and those of others leads practices to change; feedback and action are always connected. Also of significance are the dynamics that establish and alter the status of sources within environmental politics, that is, questions of change and power. There is no doubt that environmentalists can grow to become powerful, or that industries can become resource poor and culturally weak. However, that does not mean we should not continue to tackle questions of inequality, and attempt to identify routines and structures that allow power to reside more often or more fully with one or another actor in environmental politics. The chapter begins by revisiting influential approaches within media studies for thinking about power, media-source relations and news access, before turning to the sources and voices themselves; political and industry sources, and scientific and lay voices. The environment movement and its strategies are the subject of the next chapter.

News sources

Journalists, as we have seen, enact a range of practices and call upon a set of values to ensure their work meets the demands of their profession. These demands, which evolved alongside the financial imperatives of news organizations and significant social change, have been blamed for creating barriers around news, barriers that block some environmental issues from emerging onto the public agenda or from emerging in a form that allows informed and meaningful debate. Likewise, they have been seen as hindering entry into the news arena for the less powerful, allowing only elite political and social actors routinely past. In the case of mediated environmental politics and conflicts, these elites are often identified as associated with industry and government, while movement actors and the victims of environmental degradation and disasters have been labelled as the non-elite. While recognition of patterns and barriers is vital to identify the inequities that exist within public debate, we need to be able also to recognize how these are also permeable and permeated, and what entry and exit points from routines and structures exist for both journalists and their sources.

Stuart Hall and his colleagues' primary definers concept is a useful starting point for any consideration of the relationship between sources and news media. Now into its fourth decade, it remains influential despite undergoing exacting critique. For Hall, the media make comprehensible or 'map' problematic events 'within the conventional understandings' of society in two ways; they 'define for the majority of the population *what* significant events are taking place, but, also, they offer powerful interpretations of *how* to understand these events' (1978: 56, original emphasis). Implicit in these interpretations are 'orientations towards the event and people involved'. The relative autonomy of journalists undermines conspiracy theories. Rather, it is the routine structures of news production that cause the definitions of the powerful to be reproduced (1978: 57). Practical pressures mean that journalists are always working against the clock, while professional ideologies call for journalists to ground stories in 'objective' and 'authoritative' statements from 'accredited' sources, and thus structured preference – or 'over-accessing' – is given in the media 'to the opinions of the powerful'. This connects to what Howard S. Becker called the 'hierarchy of credibility'. Here, it is taken as given that members of the highest group in a ranked system 'have a right to define the way things really are' and thus 'credibility and the right to be heard are differentially distributed through the ranks of the system' (1967: 241). Hall and his colleagues dub these sources the 'primary definers' of topics (1978: 58). Any subsequent argument against their interpretation must begin from the framework provided by this primary definition, or risk being labelled irrelevant. Thus the norm of 'balance' provides little mitigation as issues have already been defined by the powerful, the problem framed, and non-dominant groups cannot easily penetrate this primary definition:

> Groups which have not secured even this limited measure of access are regularly and systematically stigmatized, in their absence, as 'extreme', their actions systematically deauthenticated by being labelled as 'irrational'. The closure of the topic around its initial definition is far easier to achieve against groups which are fragmented, relatively inarticulate, or refuse to order their 'aims' in terms of reasonable demands and a practical program of reforms, or which adopt extreme oppositional means of struggle to secure their ends, win a hearing or defend their interests. Any of these characteristics make it easier for the privileged definers to label them freely, and to refuse to take their counter-definitions into account. (Hall et al. 1978: 64–5)

Thus, the media 'help to reproduce and sustain the definitions of the situation which favour the powerful, not only by actively recruiting the powerful in the initial stages where topics are structured, but by favouring certain ways of setting up topics, and maintaining certain strategic areas of silence' (Hall et al. 1978: 65). Hall and his colleagues express several reservations with the concept: the fact that institutions can oppose each other; that the motives of the media are often different from those of the state, for example, the media want to be first with news; and that the media often wish to reveal things that primary definers would rather keep quiet. But these reservations are not expanded upon in any detail. They find that 'it seems undeniable that the *prevailing tendency* in the media is towards the reproduction, *amidst all their contradictions*, of the definitions of the powerful, of the dominant ideology (Hall et al. 1978: 65–6, original emphasis).

Herbert Gans' 1979 study of news making also finds that power is a significant factor in determining news access, but it is in a footnote that he hints at the possibility of far greater complexities:

> To understand the news fully, researchers must study sources as roles and as representatives of the organized and unorganized groups for whom they act and speak, and thus also as holders of power. Above all, researchers should determine what groups create or become sources, and with what agendas; what interests they pursue in seeking access to the news and in refusing it. Parallel studies should be made of groups that cannot get into the news, and why this is so. And researchers must ask what effect obtaining or failing to obtain access to the news has on the power, the interests, and the subsequent activities of groups who become or are represented by sources. (Gans 1979: 360)

In a seminal 1990 essay, Philip Schlesinger expands on Gans' suggestion, arguing for an approach that allows a consideration of questions about competition for space in the media by non-dominant sources from *within* a theory of dominance. Thus, while acknowledging that the organization of journalistic practice '*generally* promotes the interest of authoritative sources', he also exposes the primary definer concept and its structuralist approach to wide-ranging criticisms, inspired in part by Pierre Bourdieu's more cultural-based analysis of journalistic activity (Schlesinger 1990: 69; see also Schlesinger and Tumber 1994: 17–21). Firstly, the concept does not take into account the contestation between sources in trying to influence the definition of a story. For example, one government department may not agree with another, a plausible scenario if one considers the likelihood of conflicting views

between, say, environment and agricultural departments on irriga-
tion and water use. Which will have primacy? Who becomes the
primary definer on such a key policy question for a country like
Australia? This point then begs the question: can there be only one
primary definer? Secondly, the concept's reliance on text analysis
as a method means that behind-the-scenes negotiations, such as
off-the-record briefings by sources, remain invisible. Likewise,
it cannot 'get at' the activities of sources that attempt to generate 'counter-definitions', that is, it 'rules out any analysis of the
process of *negotiation* about policy questions between power
holders and their opponents that may occur prior to the issuing
of what are assumed to be primary definitions' (Schlesinger and
Tumber 1994: 20, original emphasis). A third criticism focuses
on the fact that the concept does not acknowledge the inequality that exists between primary definers – not all 'representative'
figures have equal access and may indeed have to strategize to
compete for news access against a more powerful figure, such
as an environment minister's office against the prime minister's.
A fourth is that longer-term issues of access and changes in the
power structure are ignored. For example, as we saw in the previous chapter in relation to climate change, the scientists who
initially dominated the UK debate lost their access and definitional
power with the politicization of the subject in the late 1980s.
In turn, the conservative sources who dominated US coverage
throughout the George W. Bush presidency found their access
reduced once the issue was acknowledged as a crisis and reinforced by the change of president. A fifth criticism focuses on the
concept's assumption of a passive media and thus sees the movement of definitions as '*uniformly* from power centre to media',
ignoring the capacity of media to challenge powerful sources and
force them to respond (Schlesinger, 1990: 63, original emphasis).
Accordingly, an uncritical adherence to the model involves paying
a price as such a structuralist approach is 'profoundly incurious
about the processes whereby sources engage in ideological conflict
*prior to or contemporaneous with the appearance of definitions in
the media*' (Schlesinger 1990: 68, original emphasis).

So while Schlesinger warns against ignoring the privileged

access of some sources, he argues that Hall and his colleagues have underestimated the level of negotiation and contestation that takes place between sources:

> it is necessary that sources be conceived as occupying fields in which *competition for access* to the media takes place, but in which material and symbolic advantages are unequally distributed. But the most advantaged do not secure a primary definition in virtue of their positions alone. Rather, if they do so, it is because of successful *strategic action* in an imperfectly competitive field. (Schlesinger 1990: 77, original emphasis)

Various other models have been developed to describe the nature and extent of such hierarchical influence. Daniel Hallin's spheres of political discourse (1986; see also Miller and Riechert 2000: 52; Allan 2004: 63–4) illustrate, as one circle inside another, how the norm of objectivity leads to a hierarchical division of source credibility. In the middle is the sphere of consensus, encircling those issues considered to be uncontroversial and beyond partisan dispute, 'the motherhood and apple pie' region (Hallin 1986: 116). Next is the sphere of legitimate controversy, which incorporates those issues believed by journalists to be valid subjects of conflict, such as elections and legislative debates. Here, reporting is dominated by the values of 'objectivity' and 'balance', the 'supreme journalistic virtues' (Hallin 1986: 116). At the outer level is the sphere of deviance, which is filled with the issues and voices that journalists consider unworthy of being heard. In this sphere, journalists maintain boundaries by excluding, condemning and exposing (Hallin 1986: 117). Thus, the further away from the centre of political consensus a source is, the less likely they are to achieve news access.

Such models remind us of structured inequities and power hierarchies, of boundaries, but analyses of source-media relations need also to be aware of where and why openings occur, of how porous some boundaries can be, and how those boundaries might shift. This is important work as it reveals the means and methods those often excluded from public debate, the non-elite political contenders and the 'voices' of the ordinary and affected, can use to enter the public arena and be heard. Research on media and environmental sources (see especially work by Alison Anderson and Anders Hansen) and media and sources more broadly (for example, studies by Simon Cottle, Aeron Davis and Paul Manning) has increasingly viewed non-dominant sources as involved in a complex struggle over news access with powerful sources, news media and each other. These studies do not ignore structural inequities and unequal distribution of resourcing that affect sources, but they are interested in the processes and practices that allow sources – elite *and* non-elite – to gain news access (Cottle 2003: 14). This chapter now turns to detailing some of the specific features at the media-source interface of environmental debate, through a lens focused on the sources and voices themselves.

Political and industry communications

Public relations activity plays a significant but not always easily visible role in environmental politics. A tendency towards reductionist or siloed accounts of this activity and subsequent news content is evident in some commentary on media and environment. In these accounts, contemporary news media are bullied and cowed by well funded, complex and partially hidden networks of pro-development interests, whether connected to industry or government, or both. Here, public relations professionals exploit willing, harried and/or lazy news journalists with highly crafted media releases or, when that fails, bullying tactics, or professional political strategists masquerading as concerned community groups ensure news balance is tipped in favour of the latest development proposal. Such commentary may feel conspiratorial at times, yet it also contains important elements that need to be considered.

There are two trends that prompt most contemporary anxiety about journalistic independence and the continuing capacity of news media to act as a 'fourth estate'. The first trend relates to what is happening within media organizations and their newsrooms. Shifts in media consumption patterns and financial demands have seen increased output on a number of news fronts, including more sections in newspapers, multiple channels for broadcasters, and integrated websites for all sectors, while at the same time, cuts to resourcing of the news gathering process have meant fewer reporters or the same number but with more to do. Related also are technological shifts that have seen layers of the news-making process disappear, decrease or move off-site, such as sub-editors in many newspapers. In their 2008 report 'Quality and Independence of British Journalism', Justin Lewis and colleagues from Cardiff University attempted to quantify and contextualize these shifts, finding that while there had been a slight increase in editorial employment in the twenty years between 1985 and 2005, editorial employees in 2005 were expected on average to produce three times as much content as their counterparts two decades earlier. In terms of newspapers, for example, *The Times, Sun, Mirror* and *Daily Mail* had all more than doubled their number of pages, while the *Guardian*'s pages had tripled (2008: 11). The journalists contacted by researchers:

> felt that there was less checking and contextualizing of stories than hitherto. This is certainly the case in terms of the finished product. Only half the stories in our press sample made any visible attempt to contextualize or verify the main source of information in the story, and in less than one in five cases was this done meaningfully. Broadcast news does better, with 42% of cases involving thorough contextualization or verification, although it is clear this is not the norm in either form of news. (Lewis et al. 2008: 4)

Overall, journalists felt that the 'pressure to produce a high number of stories daily had intensified, and that this increased their reliance on recycling material rather than reporting independently' (Lewis et al. 2008: 4). In the US, newspapers have cut at least seventeen per cent of their news staff since 2001 – 5,900 news workers in 2008 alone – but this has been accompanied recently by a loss of space devoted to news, a combination of higher newsprint prices and other operating costs. The 2009 State of the News Media report found that, 'Fewer people and less space equates to significant erosion of the serious, accountability reporting that newspapers do more than any other medium' (Pew Project for Excellence in Journalism 2009).

The second trend relates to what is happening not in news media but around them: in the public relations industry itself, in government and corporate communications offices, in organizations with resources dedicated to influencing the content of news. Here, there has been a noticeable increase in employment. Aeron Davis provides data that shows PR resourcing by UK government departments and institutions, such as the Home Office, Treasury, Buckingham Palace, the Metropolitan Police, Inland Revenue and the British Broadcasting Corporation, had increased significantly between 1979 and 2001; by 983 per cent in the case of the Metropolitan Police, where the number of public relations professionals had increased from six to sixty-five over the period (Davis 2003: 30). Other figures cited by Davis show an eleven-fold increase in corporate sector PR between 1979 and 1998; that twenty per cent of the top 500 companies as listed in the 'Times 1000' used PR consultancies in 1979, rising to sixty-nine per cent in 1984 (ninety per cent of the top 100); and that a majority of NGOs, local councils and unions had also significantly increased their PR efforts (Davis 2003: 28–30). In the US in 2000, the top twenty-five public relations companies employed over 200,000 people and received more than US$3,600 million in revenue (Beder 2004: 214). Environmental public relations has been identified as one of the fastest growing areas in the 1990s, with the amount that US firms were spending on public relations advice on how to green their image (labelled 'greenwashing') and deal with environmental opposition doubling each year in the first five years of the decade to US$1 billion (Beder 2004: 214).

In the lead up to the crucial United Nations negotiations on climate change in Copenhagen in December 2009, the US oil, gas and coal industry reportedly increased its public relations budget by fifty per cent. The spoiler campaign, which aimed to cut off support for US President Barack Obama's plan to build a clean energy economy by limiting greenhouse gas emissions, ran to hundreds of millions of dollars and involved industry front groups, lobbying firms, television, print and radio advertising, and donations to pivotal members of Congress. As the *Guardian* newspaper noted, much is at stake for many people in the US energy debate and those stakes intensified in the lead up to Copenhagen:

> But it is an unequal contest. Liberal and environmental organizations, as well as the major corporations that support climate change legislation, say they are being vastly outspent by fossil fuel interests.
>
> 'These guys are spending a billion dollars this year convincing Americans that they are clean, green, cuddly and warm,' said Bob Perkowitz, founder of the eco-America PR firm ... 'The enviros are getting their message out, but they are being outspent by 10 to one,' he said. (Goldenberg 2009: 1–2)

As this example shows, not all PR effort is directed at influencing news media content; much government and corporate activity is also put towards direct communications with stakeholders, decision makers and the public more broadly. But a lot is. News, unlike advertising or many other communications campaigns, is free and more likely to be politically influential. And news media are responsive. The Cardiff University team found that, in the UK, nineteen per cent of newspaper stories and seventeen per cent of broadcast stories were 'verifiably derived *mainly* or *wholly* from PR material or activity' (Lewis et al. 2008: 17, original emphasis). Aeron Davis describes the anxiety when the trends in journalism and public relations merge, again in a UK context:

> Clearly, as British journalism is repeatedly cut and squeezed, so standards drop and the need to cut corners becomes crucial. Journalists must do more with less resources and are becoming outnumbered and outresourced by the PR counterparts. Given this state of affairs, reporters are likely to become increasingly dependent on the steady supply of conveniently packaged (and free) public relations 'information subsidies' ... Although journalists get to pick and choose what they want to use, and they retain their conscious autonomy, they are, in effect, making reactive choices – rather than pursing proactive investigations. (Davis 2003: 32)

Sometimes – for example, in the case of industrial accidents – power in the news arena is not about being in the news, but staying out of it. Here, access is about control over the news environment. In their important work on source-media relations in Canada, Ericson, Baranek and Chan found that for 'the private corporation, power over the news is power to stay out of the news' (1989: 390). Take this quote from a public relations consultant, who has handled the account of Australia's largest and most controversial forestry company, Gunns Ltd, which continues to log old-growth forests. For the consultant, being forced by journalists to respond to stories generated by the media or other sources, such as environmental pressure group the Wilderness Society, equates to handing over power to political opponents, including news media:

> I guess a major criticism has been to say, 'Why doesn't Gunns and the industry come out and respond?' Well, they would be spending every day all day out responding and I think the shift has come that they now are not going to be responding and playing to the Wilderness Society's tune and the media's tune . . . There's been far too much power in the hands of the media. If a journalist rings up and says, 'We want to speak to them in half an hour and if they're not available we're going to run the story anyway,' then the industry has to say, 'We're sorry, we can't meet that, we'll provide you with a statement . . .'. I think the media has been too powerful and you are going to see a shift where, certainly from a communications strategy point of view, we are going to marginalize the media and say the media shouldn't be the ones calling the tunes. They should be used the way the Wilderness Society uses them. They'll be used and given information if it suits. We'll do a media conference if it suits. But just because they want to do a story today doesn't mean you have to do a story. (Quoted in Lester 2007: 126–7)

Further connections between public relations and news media become relevant when one considers the movement of journalists through various roles, both within newsrooms and beyond. Reporters on metropolitan newspapers, for example, may move quickly from cadetship to general to rounds or beats: police, courts, parliament. Others leave news altogether. Either way, gaps in experience and corporate memory emerge. Phillip Knightley notes the impact of this loss in relation to media coverage of the first Gulf War. War correspondents, he says, are not only divided and competitive, but have 'little or no memory'. They have short working lives and no means or tradition of passing on their experience, while the military is an ongoing institution that studies wars, learns lessons, devises, tests and polishes systems (Knightley 2000: 484). Many journalists who leave news media are employed in the government and corporate sectors, and – if less so – by NGOs as communications practitioners (Davis 2003: 30).

As noted earlier, the news media are not the only target of promotional activity, but they are an important one, and as such journalists are in high demand within public relations for three main reasons: they have been taught to communicate clearly, they know how newsrooms work, and they have a network of contacts within news organizations. That is, journalists are increasingly becoming sources. This is likely to impact on media-source interaction in two key ways. Firstly, it impacts the newsroom. As senior reporters abandon journalism, newsrooms are increasingly staffed by juniors. How does Herman and Chomsky's concept of 'flak' as a disciplinary measure against journalists (see Chapter Two) manifest itself when the source monitoring and providing feedback on a journalist's story is a former senior journalist from the news organization, that is, a former colleague? Secondly, journalists may come relatively cheap, but they are nevertheless beyond the financial resources of many smaller or non-elite source organizations. How does this affect news access for these groups?

Comments from one of Australia's most high profile environmental activists, Senator Christine Milne, address these concerns from the perspective of the environment movement. Milne entered public life as a campaigner against a pulp mill proposal in 1989, before becoming a member of parliament for the Australian Greens:

> The government didn't have a stable of spin doctors in the late 1980s. That is a serious crisis that has occurred in the last fifteen years. You don't get the news now; you get press releases coming from ministerial offices and journalists running them straight . . . The other big thing in the last fifteen years is the arrival of the communication companies.

In 1989–1990, journalists didn't see their career path as being into the premier's office or into corporate communications. So they were never looking over their shoulder when they wrote stories, wondering, 'Will this compromise my capacity to get into the premier's media office or will this compromise my capacity to go to a corporate media office and to take on a Gunns file?' In 1989–1990, a future career for a journalist was to become the editor of the newspaper or move up the hierarchy in the media in some form. The other problem is that it is the spin doctors who now have that corporate memory because they'd been there and the young journos have no idea and don't even know what questions to ask. (Quoted in Lester 2007: 142)

Overall, then, the substantial resourcing of public relations activities by industry and government are significant grounds for concern when combined with news media's general tendency to provide greater news access to powerful sources, a tendency known to be in part a result of news work pressures. As these pressures increase, with journalists providing more copy each day, the dominance of elite sources within news could be expected to become more pronounced. The cards seem stacked in favour of these powerful sources: against weaker sources and a weakened media. Nevertheless, a number of studies have found greater cause for optimism. What connects them is a view beyond the impact of corporate and government public relations on news media content to the behind-the-scenes activities and negotiations between media and their sources, both elite *and* non-elite. They also acknowledge that the status of these sources changes across time and space. For example, the public relations activities of Gunns, the Australian forestry company mentioned in the above quotes, will be more effective in a regional news environment than in news generated nationally or internationally (Lester 2007). Likewise, Greenpeace's status varies from country to country in which the NGO operates, and its position as source will vary depending on the location where news is generated, the type of story in which it appears, and the medium via which the story is transmitted (Anderson and Marhadour 2007).

There is no simple equation here directly correlating economic resources or institutional power with news access. Rather, and as

Herbert Gans (1979) and Philip Schlesinger (1990) predicted, the picture is complicated once a media-centric stance is abandoned. This will become evident in the next two chapters, which turn to the strategies and symbols associated with environmental politics. A further case for optimism is provided by Brian McNair, who argues that public relations activities and other attempts to manage media content within the political sphere have been 'rendered transparent (and thus subverted) by the forensic analysis of spin undertaken by political journalists' (2006: 64). Undoubtedly, websites and wikis such as PRwatch and Sourcewatch, produced by the US-based Centre for Media and Democracy, have contributed to this transparency. Stories explicitly about spin strategy and cost will also often be part of coverage of environmental conflict; for example, the coverage of the Trafigura scandal, in which British-based oil traders were accused of dumping toxic waste on the Ivory Coast, included a story about the GBP500-per-hour PR firm hired by Trafigura and its media and lobbying tactics (Leigh and Hirsch 2009: 13). McNair suggests that the exposure of PR activities has been accompanied by a general decline in deference for elite groups.

This raises further questions. Spin may now be rendered transparent, but has not a form of 'forensic analysis' always been directed against the activities of those without political authority and power, for example, against the protest activities of sections of the environment movement? Is a corrective underway or indeed has the critique of movement activities also increased? Likewise, we could ask if a general decline in deference for elite groups has been accompanied by an increase in status for non-elites, or has this decline been extended to all forms of political activity? McNair also identifies an irony:

> To communicate effectively in an environment characterized by a heightened cultural chaos (which will include the unpredictable eruptions associated with democratic politics, free market economics, and diffuse, accessible, interactive technologies) requires paying more attention than ever before to the content, presentation and distribution of the message; to the design, in other words, of effective source strategies, or public relations. (McNair 2006: 195)

In the feverish atmosphere that preceded the December 2009 Copenhagen climate talks, the conservative Australian think tank, the Institute of Public Affairs, accused Australia's mainstream media of 'pretty much' ignoring the story on the leaked 'Climategate' emails from University of East Anglia researchers, which raised allegations that the case for global warming had been exaggerated and contrary scientific opinion suppressed. The think tank claimed that the story had got twenty-five times more publicity in the US than in Australia, and 'even' three times more in New Zealand. 'It reveals the extent of group think in political and media circles,' institute director John Roskam claimed. 'I think the mainstream media has let down the Australian public by not covering this' (Weekend Australian 2009: 2). One thing is clear: whether elite or not, with shifting or stable status, what appears within the news arena matters as much as ever, if not more, in environmental politics.

Scientific sources, lay voices

Public knowledge of risks – how we become aware of them, assess their dangers, determine a course of action – is dependent, first and foremost, on the recognition of the risk as a problem. This, we know, relies in turn on successful public claims making by a variety of actors, who compete to have the legitimacy of their claims recognized in the public sphere. Given the media practices and norms that routinely send journalists to authoritative sources and the institutional housing of much contemporary scientific research, we might reasonably expect science to have a fairly straightforward role within news media as a credible source. In many respects, this is true. However, as mentioned earlier, there is also much in the relationship between science and media that is fraught, tense and unexpected, and scientists too need to compete for access. Likewise, we could expect the voices of 'ordinary' people affected by risk to be marginalized by their lack of institutional-derived authority. This also is generally the case in much reporting of environmental risk. Ordinary people may routinely appear in such coverage, but if they have a role as a news source, it is often as victims, sufferers, little more than symbolic representations of the risk itself, and without the wherewithal to promote action and change. Yet, again, 'ordinary' voices are sometimes able to break through the barriers imposed by news routines, with potentially significant effect on not only how a problem is framed and shaped for the public but with the power to create real social change.

The 1995 campaign by Greenpeace against plans by oil company Shell to dispose of a redundant North Sea oil terminal, the Brent Spar, in 1995 by towing it into the Atlantic Ocean and sinking it proved a seminal moment in environmental politics, generating vast amounts of media coverage in the UK and elsewhere and exposing the role science plays in such mediated conflict (Anderson 1997; Hansen 2000). While the campaign was successful in that it forced Shell to change its plans, the conflict also created controversy about the way scientific data were deployed to legitimize claims made by Greenpeace, Shell and the UK government, which had approved the disposal, a deployment in and of which news media were both complicit and critical. While scientific discourse was just one aspect of the controversy, Anders Hansen notes that 'science, research evidence and scientists were pressed into service by the key players . . . as well as by the newspapers themselves' (2000: 66). The role of science in the coverage was one of 'asserting facts' or 'bolstering of the arguments for or against dumping', while information about how these facts were established – for example, claims to the extent deep-sea dumping would harm marine life – was absent (Hansen 2000: 66).

This allowed the scientific data to be appropriated by the UK newspapers covering the conflict towards their ideological positions. This quote is from the *Daily Mirror*, which promoted Greenpeace's 'pollution' frame:

> Experts fear the millions of tons of steel, copper, lead and waste oil from old rigs could wipe out many species. They threaten fish stocks, seals, whales and dolphins. Greenpeace say their studies have already shown the shattering impact of pollution on marine life. (Quoted in Hansen 2000: 67)

This from the *Daily Telegraph*, which gave considerable space to scientists who supported the dumping:

> The Government and Shell say that more than GBP1 million and 30 scientific studies have gone into proving that dumping the installation at sea is the best environmental option and the safest. (Quoted in Hansen 2000: 69)

So here a scientific discourse is deployed to legitimize political claims and, in the case of the UK press, the ideological position of the newspapers. This type of coverage is not, of course, an in-depth explanation or examination of the science, and nor does it provide access to the news arena for a scientific source on the terms the source might prefer. Nevertheless, there is also evidence that as an issue becomes more newsworthy, space opens for more in-depth coverage. The formats used to cover an issue as it becomes more salient in terms of news frequency and extent of coverage will often change to become more expansive and reflexive, including more news features, background analyses and discussion formats (Cottle and Rai 2006; Cottle 2009: 79). Thus, in some cases, science may enter the news arena in a restricted form and as a political 'tool', but emerge more fully as a credible source in its own right as interest in an issue and demand for in-depth information grows.

Nevertheless, science, if not more so than other forms of knowledge, is open to negotiation, contest and controversy. For Henry Pollack, uncertain science or 'unsettled science' does not equate to unsound science: 'The normal state of affairs in science is unsettled and uncertain, and no amount of new research will completely eliminate uncertainty' (2005: 6). In the case of climate change, such 'uncertainty' allows doubt to be strategically amplified in the public's mind by those whose interests would be harmed by widespread public belief in human-caused climate change. US Republican adviser Frank Luntz's memo on climate change, during the first George W. Bush term, is now an infamous example: 'Should the public come to believe that the scientific issues are settled, their views about global warming will change accordingly. Therefore, you need to continue to make the lack of scientific certainty a primary issue in the debate' (quoted in Monbiot 2006: 27). Pollack calls such strategists and activity the 'sowers of uncertainty'.

Such attacks on the science of environmental risk can then be taken up by politicians and other decision makers, who argue that they are supported by 'sound' science, 'real' science, thereby further undermining the contrary position. There is nothing new about this – Rachel Carson's 1962 assertions about the devastating impacts of DDT were publicly derided by the pesticide industry as 'weak science', as were claims about the ill-effects of smoking, acid rain and CFCs impact on the ozone layer (Pollack 2005: 15). More recently, a common accusation made by climate change deniers against scientists who agree that anthropogenic climate change is underway is that they have much to gain by promoting a global crisis as governments will be forced to increase scientific funding. On the other hand, scientists who do not support the consensus view are accused of being 'in the pocket' of industry and governments who do not want to shift practices and policies to comply with international treaties (Hannigan 2006: 30).

Scientists, such as James Hansen in the US, David Bellamy in the UK or Ian Plimer in Australia, have become key actors in environmental politics, making high-profile interjections and/or taking clear positions in mediated conflicts. Others will describe themselves unapologetically as environmental advocates, exploiting their scientific knowledge and credentials to run environmental campaigns, sparking intense debate within the scientific community (Cox 2010: 318). For some, this politicization has undermined the role of science as a political adjudicator, able to translate complex, uncertain and conflicted scientific data. It may also create additional confusion – 'who do we believe now?' – for an already perplexed public.

However, for many scientists, news access itself is the problem, both in terms of entry into the arena to have their scientific research publicized and entering in a way that does not leave their research vulnerable to appropriation by various ideological and political positions. As Allan quoting Salisbury notes, a basic disjuncture remains between science and media that can quickly develop into a fraught relationship, based upon differing 'time zones' where scientists work for months or years on projects, with research completed months before findings are published; different regard for detail and the 'big picture'; disputation and conflict, which scientists use to build consensus but journalists use to build drama; and the use of technical terms that scientists feel builds precision, but journalists avoid (2002: 85–6).

Some science communicators have responded by attempting to establish a set of practices that allow these aims to be met within the dictates laid down by news media norms and practices. James Fahn from the Earth Journalism Network, for example, suggests that science communicators 'sell' their stories on climate change by using different angles, tying stories to interesting people, places and topics and finding a local focus (Fahn 2009). Likewise, scientists have become increasingly aware of the drivers of news journalism, prepared to accept that mutual benefits can emerge from the relationship (Allan 2002: 85). For example, ecologist Jamie Kirkpatrick suggests that the 'maximum dichotomization' of an issue that increases media exposure is both 'an opportunity and a trap' for scientists, and he recommends allowing 'your emotions to be apparent, especially in the electronic media' in order to reinforce a logical case (Kirkpatrick 1998: 40).

Clearly, mediated public debate about climate change has exposed and at times made raw the challenges for both science and news media – and the difficulties inherent in their relationship. While science has remained a key source of news on what has emerged as a crucial public policy issue of our times, it has itself become an additional site of conflict on which coverage has focused. Surveys that find the public believes that a higher level of disagreement exists between scientists on the issue of anthropogenic global warming than does in reality (Giddens 2009: 101) are further evidence of the failure of the two fields to work together to provide an accurate reflection of environmental risk to the public.

If scientific sources appeal to a public faith (albeit dented) that science can both define and provide solutions to risks – a scientific rationality – then the voices of ordinary people and their children who suffer the side effects of a risk society, such as illnesses caused by pollution or toxic dumps, could be expected to carry another sort of appeal to rationality. Robert Cox, for example, identifies a 'cultural rationality', one that 'recognizes the cultural knowledge and the experience of local communities' (2010: 199), and here we could reasonably expect 'ordinary people' to contribute as news sources. For Beck, the 'voices of the side effects' carry a form of knowledge that plays a crucial role in unveiling risks:

> What scientists call 'latent side effects' and 'unproven connections' are for them their 'coughing children' who turn blue in the foggy weather and gasp for air, with a rattle in their throat. On their side of the fence, 'side effects' have *voices*, *faces*, *ears* and *tears* . . . Therefore people themselves become small, private alternative experts in risks of modernization . . . The parents begin to collect data and arguments. The 'blank spots' of modernization risks, which remain 'unseen' and 'unproven' for the experts, very quickly take form under their cognitive approach. (Beck 1992: 61, original emphasis)

However, Beck reminds us that the competing rationality claims of different actors clash with a 'multiplicity of antagonistic definitions'. It would be a mistake, for example, to assume the form of cultural rationality carried by 'ordinary voices' is deployed only as a call for environmental action. It can also dampen and contest such calls, such as when a long-term member of the surf life saving club at Bondi claims in a softer news feature that the famous Australian beach has not changed in fifty years and therefore he sees no argument for sea-rise mitigation measures. As Beck writes, the stakes are high; the key issue is how the constructions of latent side effects are upheld or undermined, which in turn allows responsibility for risks to be assigned, and thus social conditions created where 'perpetrators are directly confronted with the consequences of their actions' (2009: 30).

News media, we know, are an important arena for the crucial contest between rationality claims, and here – as with all other aspects of source-media relations – we need to look beyond structures and routines to the complexities and contingencies found within and around news media to better understand how and in what terms some voices are heard and others excluded. Studies have found that 'voices of the side effects' tend to be marginalized in news coverage of environmental issues, although how this marginalization occurs varies across news media. A study of national US newspapers, for example, found that mainstream media such as the *New York Times* and *USA Today* relied heavily upon government and industry sources, who framed their accounts of risk in terms of official assessments and assurances of safety, and thus maintained the status quo while 'drowning out' the voices of 'the common people who live with environmental risks every day and voices of groups organized to save the environment from industrialism . . .' (Pompper quoted in Cox 2010: 215).

In contrast, a study of environmental stories on UK television news found that 'ordinary voices' – the institutionally, organizationally and professionally unaligned – formed the highest percentage of voices with news involvement (Cottle 2000). However, compared to sources from pressure groups, government and science, ordinary voices appeared most commonly in 'restricted' forms of news entry – for example, as a visual reference, rather than quoted or in live interview. When further analysed in terms of their nature of access, these ordinary voices were shown to be most commonly expressing a private and experiential account, experiences of the private sphere of self and home, rather than a public analytical account. Thus, they come to stand for the 'human side', or provide the 'human face' of environmental news stories, voices journalistically sought out and positioned to play a symbolic role, not to elaborate discursively a form of 'social rationality' (Cottle 2000: 37). There were notable exceptions, such as British mother Frances Hall's articulate challenge to the UK government over its advice on the safety of British beef during the 'mad cow disease' crisis of the 1990s, a disease which led to her son's death (Cottle 2000: 30). Yet:

Beck's 'voices of the "side effects"' are all too often rendered socially silent, notwithstanding their statistical and symbolic news presence, and they remain the discursive prisoners of tightly controlled forms of news entry and representation. To end, perhaps we should return to the rare 'example' of Frances Hall to remind ourselves of what exactly news access can mean when an 'ordinary person' manages to escape the cultural conventions of news sentiment, symbolic positioning and stunted presentational formats to elaborate a form of 'social rationality' in engaged public discussion. (Cottle 2000: 43–4)

The presence of scientists and ordinary people in news on the environment will be returned to in the final chapter, when we consider their capacity to symbolize risks associated with climate change. This, as we shall see, may be limited in the ways described above, but when combined with certain visual flows and other news sources, may also carry a powerful call for audience engagement, empathy and response. The next chapter focuses on a further source in environmental news, the environmental movement, where perhaps the prize of news access has been most vehemently contested and the struggle most keenly felt.

5

Movement and Protest

There are only so many banners you can hang before people in the media get bored. You've got to keep twisting it and twisting it. You've got to be outrageous. You've got to be unpredictable. And you've got to have imagination. (Paul Watson, founder and president of the Sea Shepherd Conservation Society, interview, 21 January 2009)

The environment movement is perhaps the grouping of political actors most adept at harnessing the power of symbolic action to overcome routine exclusion from news media. Protest, the movement has long known, can carry the prize of news entry. However, simply achieving entry is not enough. For meaningful political impact, access and visibility need to be both positive and sustained. Protest may be a key means for providing important short-term and symbolic gains for those environmentalists struggling to have their claims recognized against more powerful and resource-rich interests, including others promoting social and environmental change. Nevertheless, perceived as neither a 'rational' nor 'reasoned' interjection in public debate, protest usually provides only short-term and restricted visibility, rather than long-term political legitimacy for either activists or their concerns. Furthermore, as explicit political strategy to gain access, such interjections may lead to punishment by journalists with further exclusion from the news arena, either altogether by ignoring protest actions or through negative framing.

Like all activities conditioned to take place in the media arena, protest has been affected by significant shifts in recent times. Its symbols and forms, for example, are now commonly appropriated by elite political actors and their public relations consultants, dampening and countering opponents' messages within the news while also confusing and complicating the symbolic power of protest; Japanese whalers displaying signs, 'We're collecting tissue samples', to photographers flying over their blood-soaked decks or employees of Tasmanian logging companies protesting outside a Green party policy launch are examples of the symbolic core of protest being twisted in not always predictable directions. Meanwhile, protest and the messages it sends are increasingly called on to function across international contexts and global media flows. The internet has clearly been fundamental to these shifts, working as a potential liberator from the strictures of news media, while providing important new means of communication between environmental organizations and supporters, but also as another strategic tool deployed by political challengers to attract the attention of journalists and their mainstream news outlets. Today's 'public screens' and transnational technologies and networks may open new possibilities for protest events to become catalysts for meaningful public debate, but it is still unclear if and how such action creates real environmental and political change (DeLuca and Peeples 2002; Downey 2007; Cottle 2008).

This chapter continues the work of previous sections by focusing on one further actor and news source within environmental politics: the environment movement. It begins by considering how the term 'environment movement' can be applied in a time of widespread environmental concern and changing politics, and outlines the historical, highly reflexive and thus ever evolving relationship between media and movement. As noted in Chapter One, the movement and media interest in 'the environment' evolved together, and many of the practices and features of today's relationship echo and indeed reflect this symbiosis. An historical overview and analysis of contemporary case studies of protest provide a means to detail what has changed in the relationship, and what continues. The next chapter explores in further detail how symbols function in mediated environmental politics, with a focus on movement deployment of images and celebrity.

Environment movement

A majority of people in industrialized democracies will now declare some affinity to environmental values and aims (Tranter 2004: 186). They might participate in recycling, buy low energy light bulbs, watch 'green' lifestyle programs on TV, visit national parks and describe themselves as concerned for the environment when asked by pollsters. A large number of people will join environmental organizations, participate in rallies, vote for their local green candidates or write letters and emails pushing for political action on environmental issues. Some will work in large bureaucratized NGOs, well paid and internationally networked; others will volunteer for small, poorly resourced and unaligned groups formed to fight a single issue. Fewer, but nonetheless some, will leave their homes, face arrest or imprisonment by camping in forests or fields in the paths of bulldozers, or join the crews of ships ploughing remote seas to prevent whaling, sealing or toxic dumping. With such diversity of aims and actions, is it still possible to talk about an environment movement? And, if so, what kind of movement?

For Dan Brockington, focusing on wildlife conservation issues, the environment movement has 'ever increasing power, influence and wealth', evidenced by its successes (twelve per cent of the earth's surface is now protected, albeit to varying degrees); its size (four of the world's largest NGOs are conservation organizations, working globally and employing tens of thousands of people); the recognition it receives (UN Earth summits, Nobel prizes); and its integration of capitalist policies and values (for example, via support for the growth in national park tourism) (Brockington 2009: 14–15). For some, this power and influence undermine the notion of a 'movement' with shared values and ambitions. Witness, for example, the public animosity between Greenpeace and the Sea Shepherd Conservation

Society: 'Greenpeace is a $300 million-a-year industry,' says Sea Shepherd's Paul Watson. 'I don't want to be like that because that means you've got to be all things to all people and satisfy everybody' (interview, 21 January 2009). Comments by Geert Lovink, an academic and engager of 'tactical media' – a media of 'crisis, criticism and opposition' used by 'groups and individuals who feel aggrieved by or excluded from the wider culture' (Garcia and Lovink 1997) – also illuminate the unease often found within movement relationships:

> The professionalism inside the office culture of these networked organizations is said to be the only model of media-related politics if we want to have a (positive) impact, or 'make a difference' (as the ads call it). It's time to question the bureaucratic and ritualized NGO models, with their (implicit) hierarchies, management models and so-called efficiency. (Lovink 2002: 260)

NGOs like Greenpeace and Worldwide Fund for Nature are accused of mimicking the structures and practices of the governments and corporations that they lobby, thereby reproducing a regressive and conservative political culture. Nevertheless, it is important to acknowledge that such organizations continue – if to varying degrees and with varying foci – to stress the importance of non-commodifiable values (Carroll and Hackett 2006: 85), therefore maintaining an alignment with smaller, more poorly resourced or more radical groups and individuals. A unifying feature of the movement – one that commonly leaves it at odds with other political and social actors – must be a commitment to circumventing forces that prioritize the pursuit of profit well above the preservation or conservation of the natural environment.

It is also important to consider questions of power within broader contexts, crossing historical, political and geographic boundaries, and to recall, for example, that these large environmental NGOs began as small informal challenger groups and continue to evolve both in terms of internal structures and political standing. While some environmental groups can gain elite, institutionalized access to the heart of political and media power, experience demonstrates that this link remains tenuous.

Access is neither guaranteed nor consistent over time or space, as evidenced by the exclusion of many NGO and non-'sovereign state' representatives over the two weeks of the 2009 Copenhagen Climate Change Conference (see, for example, Australian 2009: 13; Furedi 2009: 12). Some will gain access within a regional or even national setting, but be excluded from the international stage, or vice versa. Others will remain excluded entirely, despite large support bases and formal organizational structures, if their aims are too far from or simply fail to register on the mainstream political agenda of the day. Groups within the movement compete; alliances are formed and divisions exploited. Therefore, any consideration of the environment movement needs to maintain a broad focus, one that incorporates both informal and formally organized political actors and actions, across wide historical, social and geopolitical settings, and is capable of recognizing internal tensions, tensions which may be both limiting and productive (Doyle 2009: 116).

Social movements in general are elusive in terms of theoretical containment. They may be defined as little more than a set of meanings, or as an organized effort involving a large number of people to challenge a major aspect of society from outside the political process (Goode and Ben-Yehuda 1994: 116; DeLuca 1999: 36). Nevertheless, a common feature has been a focus on media to promote their preferred images and frames (Castells 2009: 302). A popular metaphor to explain this historically forged relationship is a dance. It is useful in that it embraces notions of power, movement, complexity, dexterity, of an interaction that is sometimes sophisticated, sometimes clumsy and raw. Manuel Castells, for example, sees a symbiotic relationship existing between media and environmentalism in which the two partners are caught in an ongoing tap dance that changes tempo quickly and involves improvisation (2004: 168–91; see also Molotch 1979: 92; Gitlin 1980: 17). With its visuals of the interaction as occurring within agreed arenas and involving known steps yet still open to some improvisation, it is more apt than another popular description, tug-of-war (see Gans 1979: 117). Yet, while both invoke the brute strength and/or complex steps that may be involved, neither do justice to the array of actors that participate, let alone their scattered positioning in and around the media arena. As the work of researchers following Schlesinger (1990) reminded us in the previous chapter, the interaction does not take place in a political and cultural vacuum in which only a cohesive media and a cohesive movement participate. Public attention is a scarce resource and many groups compete for it. There is a raging battle to get on the already crowded dance floor in the first place.

The environment movement, like all social movements, wants to publicize new ideas, ideologies, and interact with the public on a deeper symbolic level, but to enter the media arena, they must often make 'recourse to extraordinary techniques' (Molotch and Lester 1975: 258). The use of such techniques is high risk as 'illegitimacy and/or incompetence among activists will be documented' (Molotch 1979: 91). Political challengers also pay the price for this type of entrance of having to 'stay in costume', with weaker antagonists only remaining newsworthy 'if they remain deviant' (Wolfsfeld 1997: 21). Negative impressions passed on through the media to the audience not only live on but can extend into related fields, framing future engagements (Halloran et al. 1970). As well, when the media perceive the movement as gaining strength through coverage, 'this coverage can be curtailed through a variety of public and self-justifications' (Molotch 1979: 91). Molotch concludes rightly that the participants move in 'response and in anticipation of one another's actions', dialectically bound. It is a dance, he writes, but 'sometimes a dance of death' (1979: 92).

Todd Gitlin, in his study of the rise and fall of the 1960s US student movement, also characterizes the interaction as one of action and response:

> As movement and media discovered and acted on each other, they worked out the terms with which they would recognize and work on the other; they developed a grammar of interaction. This grammar then shaped the way the movement-media history developed over the rest of the decade, opening certain possibilities and excluding others. As the movement developed, so did the media approaches to it, so that

the media's structures of cognition and interpretation never stayed entirely fixed. (Gitlin 1980: 22)

Gitlin's study remains unique in its analysis of the impact media coverage had on the dynamics of a movement over the movement's life and its attention to the 'precise historical experience' (1980: 22). He observed, for example, how media focus on conflict and deviance changed the nature of the organization by encouraging those members comfortable with radical rhetoric into leadership positions. These leaders, while able to fulfil the needs of the media, were unable to fulfil the needs of the membership. As primarily a youth movement in a culture that celebrated youth, the New Left was 'especially prone to the pressures and consequences of celebrity' (Gitlin 1980: 178), a point of relevance to the next chapter's discussion of celebrity, media and environmental politics. Another consequence of media coverage was a tendency to respond to the media's oversimplification of movement aims and issues with a stripping away of complexity on the part of the activists themselves. In conclusion, Gitlin warns that a 'strategically minded political movement cannot afford to substitute the commodity process of news, fashion, and image for a grasp of its own situation, a suitable organizational form, and a working knowledge of social conditions, structures, and interests' (1980: 238).

The environment movement wants to publicize its views, but the logic and professional practices of news media make them reluctant to participate in the mobilization of activist messages, and not only if they fail to adopt preferred media frames. Environmental groups are forced to strategize continually in order to find new means to circulate their preferred frames. This has commonly meant the adoption of new and creative styles of action, images and other symbolic references. It is this dexterous ability to find alternative access points into the broadcast and print news media that marks much contemporary environmental activism, and both this dexterity and media resistance are evident in the historical trajectory of the action with which the environment is most closely associated: protest.

Protest and demonstrations

Protest has long been integrated within the organizational structures and media conditioning of the modern environment and other social movements. While some parts of the environment movement increasingly work behind the scenes – researching and lobbying, for example – or through direct marketing and advertising campaigns, or winning seats on local councils and in parliaments, protest and demonstrations remain essential for those resource-poor organizations and individuals routinely denied access to the heart of political decision making. They can also be useful for those more resource-rich, bureaucratic arms of the movement, wanting or needing to re-engage their credentials as effective challengers within pressure politics. It therefore remains an important tool in the movement's overall strategic toolbox. Protests are colour, movement and noise. They can burst into the news but disappear again with as much speed, leaving only an acknowledgement of dissent and, if lucky, an image or association that lingers. While rarely enough on their own to refocus and reshape public debate or to create political impacts that last, such images can engage public sentiment. For many pushing for the protection of land or species from outside the centre of political power, this possibility is reason enough to protest.

Media have long been considered to label and frame protest events in such a way that prevents non-elite challengers from gaining political legitimacy. James Halloran, Philip Elliott and Graham Murdock's seminal study of the 1968 London anti-Vietnam War demonstration found that both press and television coverage concentrated selectively on the same aspects, which left readers and viewers with a 'generally negative impression of the demonstration and its participants' (1970: 311). Three reasons are isolated as to why these definitions tend to reflect those of the 'legitimated holders of power'. The event orientation of news is one in that it ignores underlying causes and content. This, in turn, means that journalists need to frame these events, seemingly without context, for the reader. The links the media often identify are those that will be salient and familiar to the largest number of readers as possible, and thus tend to be not at the level of underlying structures and processes but at the level of 'immediate forms and images' (Murdock 1981: 215). The role of labelling, which asserts the existence of a basic set of shared assumptions, is a second cause. A third is the presentation of events as theatre and spectacle, and thus emptied of their radical political content. Once the London demonstration was described in theatrical terms, and 'therefore both transitory and "not for real"', it became simultaneously both entertaining and capable of being contained and assimilated' (Murdock 1981: 216).

Similarly, David Waddington's comprehensive survey of studies of media coverage of public disorder, including riots in Britain and the United States, soccer hooliganism, industrial disputes and anti-nuclear demonstrations, finds a consistency across time, place and types of disorder (1992: 175). He isolates four pressures that he says stop media from 'meeting their own criteria of objectivity and balance in the coverage of public disorder': the professional and institutional definitions of what constitutes news; news values or newsworthiness; the need to include authoritative opinion; and finally the need to define the situation, that is for the journalist to frame it (1992: 175–6).

Such negative framing is not always immediate, but once established is difficult to shift. When Tasmania's environmental conflict took hold in the 1970s and early 1980s, news media were initially excited by protest events and associated arrests, but quickly became inured to them. Throughout the first decade of the conservation movement's 'direct action' strategy of taking protests to the threatened area, news media continued to cover such events, but framing shifted from one that brought the context for the action and the protesters' commitment to the fore to one that invariably labelled their actions as 'staged', 'theatre' and therefore, as Halloran and his colleagues found in relation to the London protests, 'not for real'. This occurred in an increasingly concentrated form, with news outlets dismissing each subsequent protest more and more quickly over the conflict's second decade. By the early 1990s, the main environmental organization in the state, the Wilderness Society, had abandoned direct action-style protests as journalists either a) no longer covered them or b) covered them negatively. Even physical risk and confrontation that included beatings and gunshots were placed within the context of tactical protest activity, which was broadly regarded as an attempt to manipulate the news agenda and, as such, dismissed. '38 Arrests in Light and Cameras Action at Forest Roadblock,' one headline declared, while the story described the protests as 'stage-managed from start to finish' (quoted in Lester 2007: 68).

However, the idea that media do not allow protest events to become the catalyst for meaningful discussion of broader social issues can be challenged once we look beyond the word-based elements of media texts. Kevin DeLuca and Jennifer Peeples' 2002 study of the coverage of the Seattle World Trade Organisation protests, for example, argues that most public discussions now take place via television, computers and newspaper front pages – screens – and new technologies have created both new forms of social organization and new modes of perception. Images have a premium over words, 'emotions over rationality, speed over reflection, distraction over deliberation, slogans over arguments, the glance over the gaze, appearance over truth, the present over the past' (DeLuca and Peeples 2002: 133). On today's public screen:

> corporations and states stage spectacles (advertising and photo ops) certifying their status before the public/people *and* activists participate through the performance of image events, employing the consequent publicity as a social medium for forming public opinion and holding corporations and states accountable. Critique through spectacle, not critique versus spectacle. (DeLuca and Peeples 2002: 134, original emphasis)

Likewise, Geoffrey Craig argues that 'spectacle' is integral to the production of public culture and a language of public culture, and regards spectacles 'as focal points that visualize issues and events, and generate public discourse' (2002: 51). Both studies are positive about the value of public discussion prompted by the protests. The 2000 Melbourne World Economic Forum protests, for example, were successful in the sense that media coverage tended to problematize the issues of globalization (Craig 2002: 50), while in Seattle, the attention of a 'distracted' media was gained by the symbolic violence and the uncivil disobedience, allowing the protesters' message to be 'played more extensively and in greater depth' (DeLuca and Peeples 2002: 144).

Another illustration from Tasmania: When street performer and activist Alana Beltran dressed as an angel, climbed on to a shaky tripod, and blocked a major tourism road near endangered forests in the Weld Valley in 2007, she contributed to the production of an image that carries powerful cultural resonances and has repeatedly accompanied or indeed carried national and international news and media commentary on Tasmanian forestry practices, including in such unlikely forums as the Italian edition of *Vanity Fair* magazine (see Figure 5.1). The image, which highlights both the magnitude of the threatened forests and the determination of protesters committed to protecting those forests, has lingered. Its impact was further enhanced by the fact that Beltran achieved space in the local news agenda for more than a year after she was arrested and subsequently sued for initially AUD$10,000 in damages by police and government. While only small routine court stories appeared in local newspapers each time the case was listed for hearing, these stories were often accompanied by the photograph, providing the issue with ongoing context, prominence and resonance, which the news texts themselves failed to do. Thus, by both meeting the demands of news and creating a 'lingering' dramatic image, Beltran and her fellow protesters were able to penetrate the barriers of a local media usually unwilling to circulate environment movement-sponsored messages and frames.

While media and movement clearly recognize the value each potentially has to the other and thus remain observant of the other's moves, the important word to stress here is 'potential': media only *potentially* provide legitimacy to movement values and claims, and environmentalists only *potentially* provide good copy and compelling news images. Previous chapters have considered a number of media-related factors that might impact on public awareness of and engagement in environmental issues, from ideas of nature to the values of news, as well as many of the features and activities that complicate the relationship between journalists and

Figure 5.1 The Weld Angel (Matthew Newton)

their sources. When it comes to environmental protest, it is useful to highlight what new factors may be at work, or existing factors at work in a different or more concentrated form, because it is clear that the already crowded source-media relationship 'dance floor' becomes even more difficult to negotiate when protest is involved.

The first of these factors is political impact. Protest events such as that by the 'Weld Angel' may indeed prompt some issues to obtain public status, sometimes even for months or years, but can they alter the political and cultural landscape in the long term? Do they contribute to lasting change? We know that protest provides important short-term and symbolic gains in a wide range of contexts, but we do not know if – and, if so, how – it provides opportunity for long-term legitimacy for political challengers or their concerns. Experts and institutional intervention are considered vital elements in the promotion and sustainability of an environmental issue in the public arena, and when extended over time, discourses prompted by disruptive events, whether oil spills or protests have tended to be reclaimed by powerful and political voices (Molotch and Lester 1975; Waisbord and Peruzzotti 2009). Anders Hansen, in his study of strategies employed by environmental groups to gain media access, finds while environmental groups may achieve massive media coverage on specific issues for a brief period, 'it is quite a different task to achieve and maintain a position as an "established", authoritative and legitimate actor in the continuous process of claims-making and policy-making on environmental matters' (Hansen 1993: 151). Nevertheless, we need to better understand the connection between protest and political and policy decision making before we can dismiss the impact of protest within broader contexts, and this requires research that focuses on the media strategies of activists *and* what it is decision makers do in and around media.

A second factor is reflexivity. Journalists are constantly receiving and giving feedback, altering their own actions through awareness of the activities of sources and other journalists, just as the understanding and behaviour of sources are altered by their relationship with journalists and other sources (Lester 2006b; Davis 2009). In times of heightened political conflict, this becomes more extreme with sources working harder to ensure journalists are aware of possible angles *and* consequences, altering behaviours, if only usually within the bounds of professional practices and organizational logics explored in earlier chapters. Sources will act pre-emptively on knowledge of a planned protest by political opponents, contacting editors or journalists and aiming to dampen coverage by increasing awareness of the potential consequences of certain coverage. The study of the Tasmanian environmental conflict, for example, found that reporting of protest events frequently referred critically to news coverage itself and the role played by – albeit – other journalists as observers and transmitters of the protest's aims and images (Lester 2007: 136–46). Will 'forensic analysis' of media provide, as Brian McNair has suggested, more opportunity than ever before for dissenting voices to be heard (2006: 64), or will this form of journalism about journalism make reporters more aware of professional norms and practices that have limited challenger voices in the past, and less likely to step beyond these boundaries?

A third related factor that needs to be taken into account is the tension between media and source power. Who has control of the news agenda: journalists or sources? Who sets the agenda for public debate? Who are the real gatekeepers of news? Protest, strategically deployed to harness and redirect images and ideas through media, can ignite this struggle over power. Sources battle against each other to harness or contain symbols; not only environmentalist against pro-development interests but also internally as groups, movements, industries and governments jostle to position themselves during intense periods of conflict. At the same time, media work to maintain control of the news arena. If not, media power – built in part on media's dominant role in the trade of symbols (Couldry 2000: 4) – is threatened. Overt strategy to subvert this power, such as protest actions designed solely to gain media space, may be punished by journalists with exclusion from the news arena. When placed in the context of the growth in public relations activities, which can often include better resourced symbolic power plays from sources who have previously achieved stronger news entry, we can ask whether we will see inequities between media sources further entrenched or weakened in the future.

A fourth complicating factor is the growing pressure on environmental activists to achieve symbolic gains that cross local and national boundaries, and interact with other national and transnational politics and publics. Much environmental conflict is now internationally oriented, even when – at first glance – it is seemingly firmly located geographically or culturally. Two examples relating to Australia and Japan follow. Australian woodchips are sold primarily to Japan, making Japan an important site of struggle for both the Australian forests industry and environmental activists. Thus, when the Wilderness Society and Greenpeace Australia/Pacific join forces to run a major protest against old-growth logging, they carefully select the nationality of protesters who will 'tree sit' and blog in their own languages, including

Japanese, from a platform high in a eucalypt in Tasmania's Styx Valley. Combined, the nationalities of the protesters symbolize a global concern for the future of the remote forests. Individually, each protester 'represents' a nation with potential commercial or political power over the Australian logging industry and its government backers. Australia has also led an international campaign against Japanese whaling in the Southern Ocean. So, likewise, when Paul Watson of the Sea Shepherd Society decides to form a 'delegation' from his ship in the Southern Ocean, he ensures that an Australian is among those who will board a Japanese whaler to deliver the written protest. When, the Japanese crew refuses to allow the protesters to return, the Australian government and its ships monitoring whaling activities are forced to intervene, activating international law and continuing, routine media attention.

Yet if we acknowledge the level of complexity and shifting dynamics that affect media within a single national context, how is it possible to predict or harness media from other nations, even those with similar operational and institutional systems? A comparative study of Japanese and Australian press coverage of whaling protests and International Whaling Commission meetings in 2005–6, for example, found major differences in news reporting that could not be solely explained by the oppositional roles played by the two nations in the conflict (Kudo 2008). While both countries' newspapers maintained strongly opinionated editorial stances that supported their governments' positions on anti-whaling protest activity, only Australian newspapers allowed this position to flow into news coverage, via the use of emotive language and sources. Both nations' presses, however, responded more fully to the formal and routine forums provided by the International Whaling Commission meetings, providing greater resources and coverage here than to the drama of the protest being played out in the Southern Ocean, with the exception of the Australian tabloid media. Also of interest was the Japanese government's response to the emotive Australian coverage, seeking to influence it via the appointment of a public relations manager with extensive experience of the Australian media and the production of its own protest images.

Such comparative studies of media and environmental protest are too rare; more are essential if we are to begin to understand how environmental issues and risks are promoted across geopolitical boundaries and allowed to take effect among governments, industries and publics with the power to intervene and influence environmental outcomes in their and other parts of the world. The example of the coverage of the whaling debate in Australia and Japan alone highlights some of the shifts in the production and reporting dynamics of environmental protest to which we must stay attuned. The transnational importation and movement of public relations and media expertise by resource-rich governments and industries involved in environmental conflict is a somewhat sobering counter to the influence of even the most powerful and globally oriented environmental NGOs. And we need to ask again how the appropriation of protest symbols and images within environmental politics by those opposed to the ideas and values of the environment movement may ultimately impact on the meanings and understandings associated with protest as a form of political challenge, not only across national borders but also over time (see also Lester 2006a). In Paul Watson's terms, it has been a straightforward equation: 'We've got a Hungarian on board. We get a lot of media in Hungary' (interview, 21 January 2009). It may not always be quite so simple. To continue exploring such questions, I want to now turn to a fifth factor, the impact of technological change, and ask how environmental activists have deployed the internet in relation to protest and the news.

Protest and the internet

Even into the mid-1990s, protests in remote areas faced logistical difficulties for their organizers and media covering them that no longer exist. Journalists and photographers will recount how they turned hotel bathrooms into darkrooms for processing film, lined up outside a single public telephone in a small village to file stories to a 'copytaker' back in the newsroom, even hailed down cars and offered payment to deliver film to a television station so stories could be broadcast on the following evening's bulletin. Protest organizers in turn needed to provide drama, good copy, spectacular images, but within the demands, limits and rhythms of traditional print and broadcast news media. This could, on the one hand, involve climbing mountains to erect radio transmitters; on the other, scheduling protest events to take into account a two-hour boat ride or drive for journalists back to the nearest telephone or newsroom to file before deadline. And here was the rub. News demanded events that fitted its strict schedule and values and demanding professional and technological logistics and then, as we have seen, criticized events that met their needs as managed and staged.

Thus, one reason alone for the celebration of today's communication and digital technologies. The internet and other ICTs allow environmental protest groups to communicate directly and almost instantaneously with their supporters and broader publics; providing information, growing support bases, mobilizing activities, encouraging external intervention. While once advertising or news coverage in the mass media, mail-outs of newsletters or public meetings were required to mobilize support and/or send a message to decision makers, now a mass email, Twitter message or Facebook update can be produced within minutes of key environmental events or political decisions affecting the environment, urging a group's supporters to – for example – email or even fax a politician's office or commit money to the cause. Surely, this lessens the movement's need for access to news media. However, the fact that these internet messages often carry a call to write letters to newspapers, to contribute money for mass media advertising, or to attend a demonstration or protest suggests the movement recognizes that 'old' media remain an important arena for the shaping of public opinion and thus policy, and thus protest will continue as a key means for gaining access to the news. But, even so, we could expect shifts in the way journalists cover environmental protest, given that new technologies combined with the changing forms and formats of news media liberate both journalists and protest organizers from the logistical demands of traditional news media. Surely, we could expect the greater flexibility and adaptability of new technologies and media forms to have opened more possibilities for positive framing of movement activities and aims. But have they?

The Sea Shepherd Society's media interactions and use of ICTs during its journeys in Antarctic waters to stop Japanese whaling provide an interesting case for considering this question. Journalists rarely commit to long voyages with Sea Shepherd, yet this has not prevented Paul Watson from becoming one of the world's most visible environmental activists, appearing regularly in news media in many parts of the world. Images of clashes between his vessels and the Japanese whaling fleet regularly appear up front in newspapers and on broadcast news bulletins. It is not only the quantity of media generated that is significant here; it is the quality. Media about Watson commonly reflect Watson's preferred frames, use images supplied by Sea Shepherd, and/or prominently quote Watson and his spokespeople. Headlines such as 'Whale defenders vow to press on' (Stedman 2010: 5) are remarkable when seen in the context of a set of professional practices and logics unlikely to provide legitimacy to political 'outsiders' who use protest as a means to be seen and heard.

One way he has achieved this success is by providing berths and access to stills photographers and camera crews in exchange for the right to release their images to news media. Nevertheless, in a 'world overwhelmed with images', Watson argues it is 'harder and harder to impress people', and thus speed becomes paramount. So the eight-person camera crew filming the reality television series 'Whale Wars' for US cable television station Animal Planet provides footage of confrontations for immediate transmission by Sea Shepherd, the precise amount of which has been negotiated (in minutes) prior to each summer's voyage. Watson's capacity to achieve successful news media access is largely reliant on satellite and internet technologies. In fact, in interview Watson stresses the significance of this to such a point that he reveals news media access as a primary purpose of his activities:

We could no longer, for instance, go down to Antarctica and do what we do if we didn't have a satellite link to upload. By the time we got back it would be old news and people would lose interest. We get things out within minutes. (Interview, 21 January 2009)

Watson's direct use of the internet serves the dual purposes of informing and engaging members, supporters and other interested individuals or groups by providing background information about the conflict over whaling and the organization, including detailing its celebrity supporters, while also providing a one-stop shop for journalists. It reproduces precise details of actions, such as GPS coordinates, as well as footage and quotes available for media use. Significantly, it also allows information about Sea Shepherd to circulate internationally, available to news organizations at their convenience, and across multiple locations. This is vital to Sea Shepherd's success as the conflict over whales needs to be mediated transnationally for the organization's goals to be achieved. After all, it is a transnational organization, the International Whaling Commission, which will ultimately decide the whales' fate.

Figure 5.2 Sea Shepherd and YouTube in the news (courtesy of The Mercury, Hobart)

In part, Watson has been able to achieve his news media success via a carefully managed image that hints at danger, unpredictability, but also highlights his crew's safety. He flies the black flag of piracy but remains just on the right side of the law, or in the murky grey space in between (Nagtzaam and Lentini 2008). He treads a fine line between action and theatre, symbolism and reality, celebrity deployment and anti-consumerism, and thus his actions and protests remain legitimate news in the eyes of media. But Watson's media strengths undoubtedly include his flexibility and his adaptability: flexibility to quickly capitalize on a situation as it emerges; adaptability to evolving media technologies, practices and logics. Watson needs to attract media attention without appearing to do so; he needs to be available for interviews and photographs without expressing a hunger or even interest in media coverage; he needs to put on actions that attract media without letting them know they are the audience. His use of the internet and other ICTs has been fundamental to building this capacity.

But should we be troubled by the Sea Shepherd Society's use of ICTs and what it tells us about directions in media coverage of environmental conflict? In two ways perhaps. The first concern relates to the increasing presence in news media of source-generated content, discussed in the previous chapter. Here, questions not only of reliability of information, but unequal resourcing between political actors including within the environment movement itself, are again raised. The second relates to news media demands that images generated by sources, and in particular non-institutional sources, are spectacular, depicting events dramatic enough to earn their place within news. This intersects with current debates about citizen-generated content more broadly, but we need to ask here whether this encourages movement actors to provide more and more drama, and drama that can never be described as 'theatre' or 'stage-managed'. Paul Watson and Sea Shepherd produce such drama – it is the nature of both the organization and the specific conflict – but what of other conflicts where bodies should not need to be endangered in order to gain political voice?

The Tasmanian conflict also raises interesting questions about how the internet is impacting on environmental protest and, more specifically, its mediation (see Lester and Hutchins 2009; see also Hutchins and Lester 2006). An interconnection of protest, news and the internet has been evident in all major protest events in Tasmania since 1998, when the first notable use of the internet as a protest tool occurred. Then, a protester dubbed 'Hector the Forest Protector' spent ten days on a twenty-five-metre high tree platform, in an area earmarked for logging, using a mobile phone, computer and internet connection to email journalists and politicians about old-growth forestry practices. The stated aim of the protest was publicity and the success of the event was measured not in terms of protecting the area – it was clear-felled within days of the protester being removed – but in the amount of mainstream media coverage that was generated. Likewise, five years later, in a much up-scaled version of this form of protest, Greenpeace and the Wilderness Society mounted a five-month-long campaign. The Global Rescue Station comprised a base camp and platform in a giant *Eucalyptus regnans*, sixty-five metres above the ground, on which, as mentioned earlier, activists from countries including Japan, Germany, Canada and Australia maintained a vigil, blogging on a website in their own languages, and with regular visits from well-known Australian celebrities. These celebrity visitors were recorded 'performing' at the camp, and recordings were made available on the website.

Again, it is clear that news media access was the primary aim of the action. On why the two organizations joined forces, Wilderness Society campaigner Vica Bayley's explained that they were able to produce a 'much better and much bigger story and much bigger and better spotlight on the forest', while according to Greenpeace Australia Pacific's Communications Team Leader Dan Cass:

> It's really just about giving the media access to the story ultimately. It's very much with that, although we did also engage cyber activists who were our online supporters and tens of thousands of them emailed Japanese companies. New media is increasingly important, but the mainstream media is still very much the main game of the environmental campaigns. You do the groundwork; you build the community

of opposition. That's the foundation, but then the icing on the cake is still mainstream media opinion. That's just how it is and that's okay. I mean that's where democracy looks at itself and judges its own values and priorities. (Quoted in Lester and Hutchins 2009: 588)

Here, then, the internet is a tool targeted at gaining news media attention for activists in two ways: firstly, as a novelty or 'point of difference' that journalists could write about, thereby attracting the attention of journalists and the public to the campaign; and secondly, as a means to 'spread the word' beyond the shores of Tasmania and mainland Australia via its promotion of international protesters and delivery of content to journalists remote from the protest site.

A third notable event occurred in late 2008, in the Upper Florentine Valley near Hobart, where two environmentalists from the unaligned and poorly resourced group, 'Still Wild Still Threatened', blockaded a logging road with a car body in which they lay with their arms chained to a concrete block embedded in the ground. Logging contractors responded by allegedly attacking the car with sledgehammers. No journalists or police were present. Hiding in the bush, a third protester filmed the encounter and posted it on the group's MySpace profile. The incident was available for viewing around the world within hours, and media releases from a variety of sources, including the activists themselves, other environmental NGOs and formal political representatives, quickly alerted news media to its presence. Journalists in Tasmania and interstate soon began to cover the story. Over the next fortnight, the event and the broader environmental issue of logging in Tasmania continued to feature in broadcast and online news and newspapers. This prominence forced the new premier of Tasmania, David Bartlett, to defend not only his views on the violence, but more importantly to reveal his environmental policies and views on forestry practices within mainstream news forums. Meanwhile, the environmental campaign gathered momentum as the publicity and debate triggered by the incident in mainstream news media travelled throughout an international network of activist and news websites (Hutchins and Lester 2010).

Figure 5.3 Australian loggers attack environmentalists (YouTube)

All political actors are now present in both the 'old' mass media and what Manuel Castells calls the 'networks of mass self-communication', and all seek to find bridges between the two to 'maximize their influence on public opinion' (Castells 2007: 257). Certainly, these examples show that environmental activists have not yet used the internet to liberate themselves from the practices and logics of 'old' media; as Castells notes more broadly, the political uses of the internet are only sometimes about bypassing 'old' media and more often about provoking mass media exposure (2007: 255). News media remain an important arena for the achievement of political visibility, and it is worth briefly visiting some audience numbers to understand why, although such data can be no more than a crude indicator.

Six months after the loggers' attack on the protesters in Tasmania in 2008, the MySpace video of the violence had been downloaded more than 11,000 times, while a second version of the video on YouTube, captioned as 'featured on Channel 9 news', had been played 6,603 times. Still Wild Still Threatened's MySpace site listed 384 friends, while its 'Causes on Facebook' listing had 7,595 members (Hutchins and Lester 2010). Two comparisons are useful here. The first is with visitor numbers to the sites of celebrity supporters of stopping old-growth logging in Tasmania. Singer and guitarist John Butler was a repeated visitor to the Global Rescue Station. The MySpace site of his band, the John Butler Trio, which provides links to a number of environmental organizations, has 109,960 friends, while YouTube clips of his performances have been downloaded, on average, over half a million times each. Clearly, the power of celebrity endorsement in expanding the internet's contribution to environmental campaigning cannot be underestimated, and its potential impact on mediated environmental politics is a subject of the next chapter.

A second comparison must acknowledge continuing audience and circulation figures of mainstream news organizations, whether in their broadcast, print or online forms. While it has fallen in market share, the Channel 9 network in Australia, for example, still attracts approximately one million viewers to its main nightly television bulletin, while its online news presence is channelled through NineMSN, which claims 8.2 million visits a month to its site. The influential *Sydney Morning Herald* and the *Age* newspapers, which both ran prominent stories on the Tasmanian forest violence, have a combined Monday–Friday circulation of more than 400,000, and the *Mercury*, Tasmania's metropolitan paper, has a circulation of just under 50,000. All rise by between 20 and 30 per cent on Saturdays (Hutchins and Lester 2010).

My point here is not to deny the power of the internet to transform the activities of environmental activists and other political challengers; it is clearly providing important new means of reaching supporters. For example, six months after the alleged sledgehammer attack in Tasmania, police and forestry contractors moved in to dismantle the protesters' longstanding camp in the Upper Florentine Valley. The group was able to quickly mobilize supporters using a variety of social networking platforms, including MySpace and Twitter. Forestry Tasmania was also able to justify its actions by posting a series of photographs of the camp – suggesting uncleanliness and its decrepit, unsafe state – on its website (Hutchins and Lester 2010). Nevertheless, it is undeniable that it is still through mainstream news media organizations that most Tasmanians and large numbers of people elsewhere were made aware of the event and the broader underlying issues. For environmentalists, then, the challenge to initiate a strategic move away from a reliance on news media outlets is far from over, meaning – to return to Paul Watson's comment at the start of this chapter – that environmentalists need to keep 'twisting it and twisting it'. The next chapter explores in more detail how environmentalists are doing exactly this by harnessing the symbolic power carried by certain images, events and people.

6

Symbols and Celebrities

The Queen's representative in north America was visiting an Inuit community in Nunavut, in the Arctic, when a couple of dead seals were laid out before her in symbolic defiance of a looming EU ban on seal products. With an ulu blade, a traditional knife, she bent over one of the freshly killed seals and cut along its body. After firmly slicing through the flesh and pulling back the skin, she turned to the woman beside her and asked for a taste. 'Could I try the heart?' she said.

A chunk of the organ was duly cut out and handed to Jean, who took a few bites, chewed on it and pronounced it good.

'It's like sushi,' she said, according to the Canadian Press news agency. 'And it's very rich in protein.'

As she wiped the blood from her mouth and fingers, she said she had done it in solidarity with the Inuit, including those in the community she was visiting, at Rankin Inlet, which is home to 2,300 people. They claim their way of life is threatened by the EU ban on seal products. (Chris McGreal, *Guardian*, 26 May 2009)

When the governor-general of Canada requested and ate a piece of raw seal heart she was doing far more than simply showing her solidarity with traditional Inuit hunting practices. She was, in fact, playing a sophisticated but somewhat dangerous game of symbolic power play, one that joined her political authority and celebrity with the perceived powerlessness of an indigenous community and its relationships with the environment, cultural traditions and a distant and resource-rich Europe. It was an act that also played in part on her own cultural background, gender and positioning within Canadian and international politics. Here, then, a simple public action on the part of an individual was able to carry, via a complex set of associations and meanings, a relatively clear message through the muddied politics that so often surround the environment. Whatever Michaëlle Jean's intent, its result was news coverage in Europe and around the world that highlighted the impact on the Inuit of the proposed EU ban on the import of seal products, as well as markedly increasing the governor-general's international profile.

What was also at play and made Jean's participation in the ritual seal butchering particularly noticeable within the increasingly crowded world of celebrity environmental politics was not only the unusualness of the act and the vividness of the images it produced, but the willingness of a well-known figure to identify herself with a position in opposition to the symbolic power of the environment movement. The US-based NGO People for the Ethical Treatment of Animals (PETA) has led and is broadly representative of movement views and responses on the issue. While not directly fighting indigenous hunting rights, PETA is opposed to the ninety per cent of the Canadian seal fur trade it claims is not related to indigenous hunters, and has pioneered the deployment of celebrity to promote its cause, most notably in its 'I'd rather go naked than wear fur' and associated protests and campaigns, which continue to attract actors, models and sports stars willing to undress and appear in print and billboard-based advertising. Combined with 'thorough investigative work, congressional involvement, consumer boycotts, and international media coverage', celebrity involvement has allowed PETA to work towards 'educating policymakers and the public about animal abuse' (PETA 2009). In a bid to stop the fur trade, PETA therefore trades heavily in images and symbols, representation, emotion and authenticity, a trade that Jean sought to challenge by deploying some of the trade's own logics and demands.

Such challenges are rare; few high-profile individuals are willing to risk their hard fought for public identities by associating themselves with environmentally unpalatable causes, even in the face of harmful impacts on local indigenous communities, and few individuals carry the strength of meaning, of authenticity, necessary for such challenges to succeed. But, just as significantly, few are willing to risk associating themselves with highly politicized or radical environmental causes, which the public has not yet or is unlikely to recognize as issues demanding policy change. Here the dangers are as great, and the demands for a robust public identity are as strong. What this might mean for environmental politics, the area of contemporary politics perhaps most infused and affected by symbolic power plays, celebrity, image and spectacle, is important to understand as it affects how public debate and policy about the environment is shaped and engaged into the future. This chapter begins by outlining the role of symbols and images in environmental politics, considering how certain images now commonly associated with environmental risk and values appear in news coverage. It then returns to the Tasmanian forests conflict to illustrate how a single tree and its death can come to symbolize widespread forest destruction and mobilize through news media national and international support. Its final focus is on the increasing presence of celebrities in news media coverage of environmental issues and their potential impact on political and physical landscapes.

Symbols and politics

Some symbols have become inseparable from contemporary mediated environmental politics; a seal cub on blood-stained ice, the bleeding body of a whale reddening icy southern waters, a pelican coated in oil, chimneys spewing pollution into darkened skies, smoking stumps, dried river beds and palm trees thrashed by hurricanes. Here, often removed from their original contexts, they can come to symbolize human destructiveness, a world in crisis, a demand for action. Images of untrammelled nature also work powerfully; their prevalence in advertising for everything from shampoo to breakfast cereals to holiday destinations alone is evidence of their perceived capacity to make us yearn for environments and landscapes undamaged by human activity, for lives less susceptible to human-made risks, for the 'natural'. But symbols also circulate in subtler, less certain, forms, working and deployed by political actors in the news arena in complex ways to promote some ideas and understandings, perhaps even calls to action, but also to reinforce established barriers to widespread participation in meaningful public debate.

Symbols shift over time and context. For example 'wilderness', as outlined in Chapter One, can in less than two decades move from signifying a barren and empty place to one that is desired, invaluable, in urgent need of our protection. The conditions that contribute to such a shift are social and political, and – as we have seen – are therefore open to contest. The symbols themselves become a key focus within environmental conflicts, as political contenders struggle to harness or contain their potential power. This is a battle that, as Ulrich Beck notes in relation to climate change, is vital for the recognition of and response to environmental risks:

> ecological images and symbols are by no means scientifically confirmed as intrinsically certain knowledge. They are culturally perceived, constructed and mediatized; they are part of the social knowledge 'fabric', with all its contradictions and conflicts. The catastrophic consequences of climate change must, as we have seen, be *made visible*, that is they must be effectively staged in order to generate pressure for action. (Beck 2009: 86)

The interplay between news media and symbolic power is never certain, yet the potential gains that come with harnessing this power are so great that all political actors are obliged to try. The unpredictability also makes it an especially attractive space for those poorly resourced and non-elite political actors attempting to challenge and circulate their messages from outside a position of primary definition or institutional dominance. Symbolic power is the ability to 'engage, influence, intervene and affirm via symbolic forms' (Thompson 1995: 17). It may also, as a more general, pervading power, construct reality (Bourdieu 1991: 166; see also Couldry 2000: 4). Pierre Bourdieu stresses that symbols are the 'instruments *par excellence* of "social integration"': as instruments of knowledge and communication . . ., they make it possible for there to be a *consensus* on the meaning of the social world, a consensus which contributes fundamentally to the reproduction of the social order' (1991: 166, original emphasis). Symbolic power, therefore, is:

> a power of constituting the given through utterances, of making people see and believe, of confirming or transforming the vision of the world and, thereby, action on the world and thus the world itself, an almost magical power which enables one to obtain the equivalent of what is obtained through force . . . (Bourdieu 1991: 170)

Symbolic power is not simple to mobilize successfully. Symbols shift; meanings shift. Sometimes political actors prompt the shift, sometimes they simply monitor and adapt, but they must always treat symbols with care as misuse or overuse can see potentially powerful symbols dissipate into meaningless images or negative rhetoric. In their public arenas model, Stephen Hilgartner and Charles Bosk highlight the importance of this in maintaining issues as social problems, arguing that if 'symbols used to frame a problem become too repetitive, if they come to saturate the prime public space, then either new ones must be found or the problem will usually undergo a decline because of its diminished dramatic value,' (1988: 62–3). This, of course, implies that the problem itself has eased or 'sheer boredom with that particular public drama may enable competitors to take its place' (Hilgartner and Bosk 1988: 62–3).

Powerful images, strong rhetoric, symbolic acts; these help to weaken the boundaries and barriers that – as noted in previous chapters – journalistic routines and norms can construct against political challengers. Symbols are thus the weapon of choice for the environment movement. Ulrich Beck calls Greenpeace, for example, a 'veritable forge of political symbols in which cultural transgressions and symbols of transgression are produced' (2009: 99). However, it would be misleading to view symbolic power as the sole domain of resource-poor, political challengers, as the governor-general of Canada was able to show. The image of a dying crested cormorant supposedly choked by an Iraqi-authorized oil slick in Kuwait is an example of symbolic power wielded by the US and UK leadership (Knightley 2000: 497). Such mediated images rely on a complex interplay between the 'real' and the 'symbolic', and an understanding of this connection helps explain how certain symbols and images come to powerfully represent and indeed construct environmental concerns and thus politics. Turning our focus to photographic images helps to illustrate the interplay.

Images of nature and the environment are political. They interject in contemporary debates; they influence opinions; they shape and contest. However, their power in the political realm is garnered largely from their trait of appearing precisely the opposite, of being non-political. More than many forms of mediated communication – and despite growing awareness of digital manipulation and/or strategic deployment by various political actors – photographs continue commonly to perform the role of iconic representations of what actually is. They rarely seem to be asking outright for the viewer to make complex connotative connections, although as communicative acts embedded within social, cultural and political contexts, this is exactly what they are always doing. It is this dual role of appearing to denote what is while also symbolizing what might be that provides them with a central place in mediated environmental politics.

Gillian Rose reminds us, simply, that 'images themselves do something' (2001: 10). David Deacon and his colleagues put it this way. The real force of the photograph lies in its iconic signification, they write:

> This force becomes even stronger when the iconic moves into the realm of the symbolic. Because iconic signs transfer into symbolic modes of signification without losing their sense of the tangible, social myths rooted in iconic/symbolic combinations are that much harder to contest than myths based entirely within the realm of the symbolic. (Deacon et al. 2007: 196)

This power has led to the image playing a foundational role in the environment movement, as it emerged in an identifiable form in nineteenth-century United States, concerned principally with the preservation of 'wilderness'. Photography played a key role in establishing the new set of meanings attached to the term, on which early environmentalists in turn shaped their political campaigns. The landscape photography of Carleton Watkins was instrumental in the 1864 preservation of Yosemite and Mariposa Big Tree Reserve in California, with photographs of the area influencing the US Congress to create the world's first wilderness park (DeLuca and Demo 2000: 254). However, in their depiction of a pristine expanse with no evidence of human activity, Watkins' photographs also helped to establish a compelling, if not necessarily 'real', vision for the environment movement and its political activities. To Kevin DeLuca and Anne Teresa Demo, this view of nature 'set in motion the trajectory of environmental politics for its first one hundred years', which created a narrow focus on protecting pristine places and delayed the emergence of a movement concerned with protecting less pristine places and 'critiquing the practices of industrialism that degraded the general environment' (2000: 257). The photos did more than represent reality. Rather, they constituted 'the context within which a politics takes place – they are creating a reality' (DeLuca and Demo 2000: 242).

A broadening of concerns within environmental politics occurred in the late 1960s and, as also mentioned earlier, it was another set of photographs that is now commonly acknowledged as contributing to that shift. The images of the earth collected during the Apollo space missions, beginning with 'Earthrise' in 1968, are believed by many to have changed human perceptions of their planet, prompting a 'reformed view of the world' (Cosgrove 1994: 273). Widely published in the news media, the images soon became mainstays of advertising and publicity copy, the emblem of choice for media, transport and communications companies wanting to associate themselves with the marvels of modernity and the power of the US space program (Cosgrove 1994: 280). But they also emphasized the earth's vulnerability; as Denis Cosgrove writes, via an 'emphasis on the loneliness of the Earth in the blackness of space', signifying the 'necessity of planetary stewardship' (1994: 287). Four decades after the Apollo missions, these two readings of the images they produced continue to circulate: within single television news bulletins, the globe can appear both as a symbol of the power of modern communications (within a bulletin's opening sequence, for example) and to represent the earth's vulnerability (as backdrop to the introduction of an environmental story) (see Cottle 2009: 85; Lester and Cottle 2009: 927).

Attempts to harness the power of the image have been a dominant motif of modern environmental politics. In Australia in the early 1980s, a photograph of a section of the threatened Franklin River, Rock Island Bend, became ubiquitous, appearing on movement-circulated postcards, posters and ultimately within political advertising. The Wilderness Society, which organized the campaign against the river's proposed damming, ran the photograph as a powerful double-page colour advertisement in the nation's largest broadsheets on the eve of a national election, with the caption 'Could you vote for a party that will destroy this?' Yet, outside advertising it was a type of image rarely seen within news media, dismissed by editorial decision makers for the political strategizing behind its creation and circulation, its inherent 'political-ness'. For recognition by and in the news, these images of pristine wilderness or wild habitats worthy of protection needed to become backdrops only to more newsworthy events (Lester 2007: 98–106).

Greenpeace had clearly recognized this by the time it emerged as a force in environmental politics in the mid-1970s. While the photograph was central to achieving its campaign goals, the images it generated did not focus on threatened places or species, but on the human endeavours to protect the places or animals. It described these endeavours, captured by the organization and circulated via the world's media, as 'bearing witness'. According to founding member Robert Hunter, 'We wanted to make the entire world witnesses, to fix an image in people's minds' (quoted in Boettger and Hamdan 2001: 13). But rather than bearing witness to ecological destruction, the images focused on acts of resistance, political acts. By doing so, Greenpeace was able to produce photographs that satisfied the criteria of news organizations for 'the ultimate picture' that is – as one newspaper editor has said – 'the frozen moment, the essence of an event, captured as it actually happens. All . . . must meet the demand they present events in an interesting and completely honest way' (quoted in Whelan 1993: 13). At the same time, Greenpeace was able to further its political goals by symbolizing the commitment of the movement and the individuals within it, and the lengths to which they were prepared to go for their cause.

As with all forms of political communications, the messages carried by such images are continually contested. However, the iconic qualities of photographs, their claim to represent the 'real', means that counter-positions often have to work harder or more creatively to succeed in the symbolic hothouse that is environmental politics. How, for example, does one contradict the meaning embedded in the image of a lone polar bear balanced on an ice floe? The image shows only that; a polar bear on a piece of ice. Yet it clearly has come to symbolize the destructive potential of climate change. Arguing against the connotative qualities of a powerful image is a weak tactic and doomed to fail, particularly while uncertainty remains in the science about the size and trajectory of polar bear populations (see Chapter Three). Similarly, the meaning of images of billowing smokestacks, coal-fired power stations and traffic on freeways is clear for most Western viewers and does not call upon complex cultural connections for the activation of symbolic meaning or power; climate change is a human-created crisis that requires a human response to avert. Such connotations may be politically contested – both science and industry groups have complained, for example, that using visuals of steam emissions from cooling towers is misleading (see, for example, Royal Society of Chemistry 2007) – but such associations continue to reverberate culturally.

Perhaps a more successful method for limiting the power of an image in environmental politics is by providing alternative images and/or contexts for images, close to the originals but capable of creating different connotative outcomes. This can be achieved by simply shifting the context of the image's publication or by changing the textual anchoring, such as captioning, of the image. So, for example, an image of a protester buried up to his neck in the path of a logging road might symbolize vulnerability and commitment in the context of an activist website; conflict provocation in a news context; and economic hardship and obstruction in the context of forest company publications (see DeLuca 1999; Lester 2007). Likewise, the photograph of a mountain with its top removed for coal mining could stand for greed and destruction in a magazine article about excesses of Big Coal; for might and power in a magazine article about the industry's successes. Sometimes, images may change context but continue to rely on previously established symbolic connections: photographs of pristine wilderness are now regularly appropriated by the tourism industry, forestry companies, water regulators, bee-keepers and others who trade on the fact that such images connote no human industry and activity (Lester 2006a). Over time, such deployment can lessen the political power of the symbol, as has occurred with the concept of 'wilderness' in many regions (Lester 2007: 109–13). This is a not dissimilar process to that which has led to the once powerful discourses of nature now being regularly appropriated for commercial gain and, ironically, to encourage greater consumption (Hansen and Machin 2008: 792).

The effectiveness of some environmental images may also be limited by their own power. For example, Julie Doyle (2007) has shown how Greenpeace's promotion of some climate change visuals, including those that provided early photographic evidence of impacts on Antarctic ice, could hinder the NGO's mobilization of support for action on climate change. 'The moment climate change can be photographed is the moment it becomes visible as a symptom . . . and thus too late for preventative action,' she writes (2007: 146). In contrast, more recent attempts by Greenpeace promote 'credible solutions' via an emphasis on decentralized sources of energy. The shift is one from 'fatalistic images' that operate to disempower human agency, to a 'more hopeful narrative based upon climate change solutions rather than one of catastrophe' (Doyle 2007: 147). These findings are supported by O'Neill and Nicholson-Cole, who argue that deployment of such images also risks resulting in 'generating rather tokenistic and general concern that operates at arm's length from the individual'. They call for research that concentrates on 'how a much deeper personal concern and lifestyle engagement with climate change can be encouraged through different methods and strategies of communication' (2009: 376–7). The potential of climate change visuals to engage and promote environmental citizenship within the specific context of news media formats will be further considered in the next chapter.

Staging of news events is, as noted earlier, a popular if unpredictable form of symbolic powerplay. Protest visuals will normally carry a set of connotations, of wanting to be heard from outside the political centre, of non-elite political status. Within environmental politics, it is usual to associate such visuals with the environment movement, the 'outsiders'. However, it is now common for industry and other groups to adopt protest events as a means to counter the growing power of the environment movement and the perceived financial and/or cultural threat created by environmentalism (Lester 2006a). This plays on social understandings of protest as the realm of the powerless, as the only means of access to the heart of democratic processes, and can work even when the connections to the core of political and economic power are known (Lester 2007: 118–23).

Thus, to understand the career of environmental issues through the news media, we need to stay attuned to political strategy but also to symbols, and – importantly – how they may work together. We need to be aware of successful power plays and failures. To further explore the role of the symbolic in contemporary environmental politics, and its manifestation in and through the news, the chapter now turns to a detailed analysis of the case of 'El Grande', which reveals how the symbolic power surrounding the tree and its death was variously exposed, suppressed and carried via the news.

Symbolizing forest destruction

Since its establishment in 1976, the Wilderness Society – Tasmania's most active and high profile environmental organization – has displayed an astute awareness of the need to harness the power of particular images, events and places. As noted above, a photograph of a small island known as 'Rock Island Bend' came to represent the travesty of flooding the Franklin River in the state's now World Heritage-listed wild south-west; in 1986, Wilderness Society leader and member of parliament Bob Brown, by placing himself under the blades of a massive excavator clearing forests at Farmhouse Creek, came to stand for the anger and sacrifice of all protesters; and, in 1995, the Aboriginal word 'Tarkine', applied by Brown to the previously unnamed area of the isolated and threatened north-west region and playing on resonances surrounding indigenous occupation, recalled the historical and cultural significance of the region. Most recently, the image 'Weld Angel' – as shown in the previous chapter – has come to symbolize not only the loss of old-growth forests but the continuing commitment of environmental campaigners. The Tasmanian news media have often shown initial resistance to using these movement-sponsored symbols, but have adopted many of them over time. In short, the power of these images and terms when combined with the professional practices and logics of journalism – for example, the desire for a single unifying name for a region increasingly featuring in news coverage – eventually overrode reluctance by news media to participate in the circulation of these symbols (Lester 2007: 93). That the environment movement in Tasmania has, at times, achieved symbolic power is a significant feat in a state with a conservative news media with strong historical ties to industry and government.

Even within the political context of media resistance in mobilizing symbolic forms, the capacity of the Tasmanian environment movement to gain symbolic power should have reached an apotheosis in 2003 with events surrounding the tree, El Grande (see also Lester 2010b). Giant trees have always been widely celebrated and mythologized, their physical presence inspiring awe, even worship (see Schama 1995; Neuzil and Kovarik 1996: 53–60; Edwards 2003). As Tim Bonyhady writes: 'Their size and age makes them one of the most patent manifestations of the wonder of the world' (2003: 5). They have been identified, measured, listed and named, with a specific language of majesty attached. Edwards notes the tradition surrounding these lists and namings:

> Ancient trees, for instance, have long earned the sobriquet 'Methuselah', while the tallest are 'patriarchs' and 'mothers of the forest'. Occasionally, as emblems of patriotic self-esteem, the grandest and most famous trees are named after national heroes and identities in the manner of California's 'General Sherman' and 'General Grant' trees, giant sequoias both. In a novel display of nationalistic ambivalence, Australia once boasted not only an 'Uncle Sam' tree but also an 'Edward VII' tree, colossal specimens of blackbutt and mountain ash respectively, that were tourist destinations near the Black Spur in Victoria until their eventual demise in the late nineteenth century. (Edwards 2003: 8)

In Tasmania, the biggest, the highest and the fattest have had names bestowed upon them by a range of the awe-inspired, including, among others, those involved in their logging (see Bonyhady 2000). El Grande was one such tree, a *Eucalyptus regnans* or swamp gum discovered in 2002 and found to be 79.5 metres high and 595 centimetres in diameter and with a total volume of 439 cubic metres. This made it Australia's largest tree and the world's largest flowering plant. Located in the Florentine Valley west of Hobart in an area earmarked for logging, it was found by University of Tasmania geologist and Wilderness Society member, Wally Hermann, who was hoping to stop logging in the area by identifying trees that qualified for protection under the Giant Trees Policy. Hermann reported the discovery of the tree to Forestry Tasmania on behalf of the Wilderness Society, but its name came from within Forestry Tasmania itself, when it was subsequently listed on the Giant Trees Register.

With old-growth logging developing as a key issue in the forthcoming state election, the Wilderness Society released details of the tree to news media. The *Mercury*, Tasmania's only metropolitan newspaper and – based in Hobart – the closest daily to the tree's location, ran a front-page picture story noting the tree's discovery and drawing attention to the unusual cooperation over

Figure 6.1   El Grande 2002 (© Wally Hermann 2002)

its measurement and protection between Forestry Tasmania and the Wilderness Society in both the headline 'Foes measure up for giant' and the introduction, 'The Wilderness Society has praised Forestry Tasmania for its swift action in protecting a giant eucalypt in the Florentine Valley' (Mercury 2002: 1). Here, El Grande was clearly allowed to perform the role of catalyst to a broader discussion of the Tasmanian environmental conflict, its discovery being framed as a symbol for 'cooperation' between the contesting sources. This would be the last time El Grande made the front page of its local newspaper, and the only occasion when its place within the broader conflict was explicitly articulated in coverage in the *Mercury*.

On 15 April 2003, ten months after El Grande was celebrated in the *Mercury* for its unifying role, Forestry Tasmania issued a 250-word media release. Under a heading 'Florentine Giant Stands Tall', it began:

Derwent District Forest Manager Steve Whiteley said today that Tasmania's largest hardwood tree, 'El Grande', has once again demonstrated the natural resilience eucalypts have to fire. 'A regeneration burn conducted earlier this month has impacted on the tree despite our efforts to protect it by clearing away nearby harvesting debris, forming fire breaks and wetting down the tree.' Mr Whiteley said the giant Florentine Valley tree had sustained charring to the trunk and part of the inside lower portion and it is expected to shed its current covering of leaves before new leaves began to shoot. 'El Grande has endured many similar challenges by wildfires in its 350-year history and once again it continues to stand tall. The *Eucalyptus regnans* is of course protected from harvesting under our Giant Tree policy.' (Forestry Tasmania 2003a)

The *Mercury* was the only news outlet to pick up the release. It ran a 141-word story the following day at the bottom of page seven, with the heading 'Tasmania's Top Tree Survives the Flames' (Mercury 2003: 7). All the information in the story was sourced from Forestry Tasmania's media release. It also ran a single column photograph of the tree, with a caption that described the tree as 'a survivor'.

The tree had, in fact, been severely damaged in the Forestry Tasmania burn-off. This was confirmed by consultant botanist Alan Gray, who inspected the tree on behalf of the Wilderness Society on 27 April. His findings were subsequently released by the organization, and nationwide publicity followed. On 1 May 2003, the story ran on the front page of the *Sydney Morning Herald*, 'Fury as Nation's Biggest Tree Goes up in Flames' (Darby 2003: 1), and page three of Melbourne's *Age*, 'Giant Tree Damaged During Burn-off', in which Greens Senator Bob Brown was quoted comparing the fire to blasting at a Sydney demolition site and saying 'woops, we got the Opera House as well' (Darby with AAP 2003: 3). The *Mercury*, the newspaper closest to the tree's location and thus, one would expect, with proximity operating strongly as a news value, picked up the story again on the same day and, again, it ran briefly at the bottom of page seven. This story implied that its initial coverage had not been completely incorrect, with the tree only 'scorched', a point reinforced both in the headline 'Doubt Cast on Scorched Tree' and introductory copy:

> Will the fat tree live or die? Two weeks ago El Grande, Australia's biggest tree, was scorched in a Forestry Tasmania regeneration burn. Forestry said the 350-year-old would survive after measures to protect it failed to stop flames licking up one side of its massive trunk. But after a visit to the Florentine Valley near Wayatinah, Paul Smith – a former forester with the company for 25 years – said he feared the eucalypt was fighting against the odds. Only spring will tell for sure. (Paine 2003a: 7)

Here, then, a story that had become front-page news in major newspapers elsewhere in Australia was given minor treatment in Tasmania's only metropolitan and politically most influential newspaper. It ignored the broader context of the issue – the continuing and bitter environmental and political conflict – thus denying the environment movement any symbolic gain. That the movement had strategically acted to not only initially find and identify the tree, but also to subsequently confirm its death, shows the movement was acutely aware of the symbolic power that could potentially be gained through the tree. However, the newspaper kept the story contained within a 'novelty' news frame, ignoring the more obvious values of proximity and conflict, and within Forestry Tasmania's preferred frames. This dynamic was sustained as the tragedy of the tree continued to unfold.

Over the following days and weeks, national and international coverage of the tree's fate grew, including coverage in the nationwide *Weekend Australian* (Altmann 2003a: 5) and on ABC radio, television and online (ABC 2003). Internationally, coverage included BBC News (BBC 2003), whose story then circulated widely among news outlets in a number of countries as well as online, and in *The Observer* and *Guardian Unlimited* (Pritchard and Townsend 2003). In Tasmania itself, the *Mercury* conceded the incident had been more than a scorching, with a page three, 450-word lead story, 'Giant Tree "Cooked to Death"' (Paine 2003b: 3). Letters appeared for some months in newspapers across Australia, including this typical one from a local correspondent in

Figure 6.2   El Grande 2003 (© Geoff Law 2003)

Wollongong's *Illawarra Mercury*, under the heading 'Wasteland', which clearly places the death of the tree within the context of the broader environmental conflict:

> The Tasmanian Government is spending $105 million on a Sydney-to-Tassie ferry to attract tourists while at the same time it is destroying Tasmania's unique tourist attractions. A few weeks ago Forestry Tasmania managed to kill the largest flowering plant in the world with a post-logging regeneration burn. El Grande, as that enormous Mountain Ash tree became known, is just one of millions of tonnes of old-growth trees mowed down in Tasmania for the export woodchip market. If you wait until the ferry service begins it may be too late to see many of these majestic Tasmanian forests. (Ryan 2003: 19)

In mid-July, 3,000 people marched against forestry practices in rain and light snow in the Styx Valley, the *Australian* reporting that 'to walk between these giants is to enter a dense Tolkienesque world of ancient, towering trees that loom up wide and high' (Altmann 2003b: 11). The national weekly news magazine, the *Bulletin*, ran a long feature on El Grande's demise in August, with the introductory text establishing the tone: 'A tree fell in Tasmania – and the world heard. The magnificent gum was alive in the time of King Charles II and had seen in the computer age only to perish under man-made flames. Vale El Grande' (Beale 2003). The mythic, celebratory language of the big trees was now mainstream; El Grande was functioning as a powerful symbol; and the movement's message was clearly circulating in interstate and international forums.

El Grande was confirmed dead by Forestry Tasmania in late 2003, prompting more stories across the country and internationally. A number of prominent longer stories and features investigating Tasmania's forest practices also appeared. In sum, the Wilderness Society had – outside Tasmania at least – mobilized the life and death of El Grande into a symbol for the destruction of Tasmania's forests, an achievement not lost on its discoverer Wally Hermann, who described the tree as 'a mighty lever in shifting human awareness, and I thank it for its huge contribution' (quoted in Beale 2003). Nor was the symbolic importance lost on journalists attempting to cover the Tasmanian forestry debate for readers outside the state.

> Forestry can be an enormously complicated story to cover. I have still got to explain to people what the RFA [Regional Forests Agreement] is and once you start introducing initials into stories like RFA, people immediately start to cool down on things when they're reading. Forestry is more complex to explain. That's why something like El Grande was a ready symbol. (Andrew Darby, *Age* and *Sydney Morning Herald*, interview, 1 December 2004)

The potential strategic significance of the tree's symbolism to the movement became clear in mid-December 2003 when a controversy over the practice of naming individual giant trees was aired in the *Mercury*. On 9 December, the Wilderness Society issued a media release responding to Forestry Tasmania's confirmation of the death of the tree. It finished with a note in parentheses: 'Note that it [El Grande] is still listed at the top of the list – but without its name' (Wilderness Society 2003). The *Mercury* followed with a story on 15 December, prominently displayed on page seven with the headline 'Giant Trees Lose Names', in which a clear connection was made between the naming practice and public attachment to the trees, and to the 'public relations disaster' of El Grande (Rose 2003: 7). Forestry Tasmania's general manager Hans Drielsma was quoted as saying 'the removal of the names was done in a routine website update' and 'was not a decision made at policy level' (Rose 2003: 7). Later that day, Forestry Tasmania's then managing director Evan Rolley issued a media release saying that the 'popular names for the Giant trees will be retained and promoted' (Forestry Tasmania 2003b). Popular names were reinstated for all but five of the twenty giant trees listed on the Forestry Tasmania website (2005a, 2005b). An asterisk appeared beside El Grande's listing pointing to a footnote, which read simply: 'The El Grande tree is dead.'

This detailed account of El Grande's demise as told by and through the news media clearly reveals the contest at the heart of environmental conflict for symbolic power. As discussed in the previous chapter, the four-decade-long Tasmanian conflict has been marked by restrictions on news entry for the environment movement if its strategic intent becomes too overt. Analysis of the El Grande coverage reveals similar complex dynamics at work, and these gain even more analytical clarity when the media are seen as active agents in the contest, the conflict as 'mediatized' (Cottle 2006). In short, by suppressing the coverage of El Grande and thus disallowing the movement's strategic intervention, the media maintained control of the news agenda in Tasmania. This control is over more than symbolic power, it is for media power, and it is a struggle in which the media have a core interest and are active participants. Forestry Tasmania was able to maintain a definitional advantage, not solely because of its public relations activities – which at their best were crude and at their worst misleading – but because of the active intervention by local media to stop symbolic power transferring to the environment movement. The movement's message was harnessed and contained by journalistic practices not to support the interests of elite sources but seemingly to prevent the movement from strategically gaining control of the news agenda and from gaining symbolic power, the power to 'engage, influence, intervene' (Thompson 1995: 17).

This leads us to ask about the impact of an increasingly global media and political environment on these dynamics. The strategic intervention of the Wilderness Society in events surrounding El Grande were not seen by national or international journalists as detracting from the newsworthiness of the story as a whole; these media were not concerned with containing the symbolic power of the Tasmanian environment movement. They ignored the initial local framing of the story, and likewise local media did not follow interstate or international framing. This reminds us that despite an increasingly globalized communications environment, we need to stay attuned to the specifics of local media and politics. National and international opinion has clearly impacted in the past on Tasmania, most notably in the case of the Franklin River campaign when the federal government invoked its international treaty obligations to stop the dam, but this relies on an alignment of media coverage and public opinion with electoral cycles and political willingness to intervene in local affairs. The environment movement cannot afford to operate only on this level while environmental futures are being determined locally. Media and political dynamics continue to matter at this highly localized level.

Increasingly, media theorizing allows space for stories keyed in to the symbolic to actively challenge institutionalized elite power and deepen democratic and other public participation. As this example has shown, we do, however, need to stay highly attuned to the complex processes at play in the relationships between public relations and news media, words and images, local stories and global flows, and the images and symbols at play within single news items as well as in the coverage of an issue as a whole. Celebrity, as the next section shows, introduces yet another set of contingencies into the relationship between symbols, images, movement politics and news media.

Celebrity protesters

Paul Watson, of the Sea Shepherd Conservation Society, knows the value of celebrity support within the symbolic powerplay of environmental politics:

> Lots of celebrities support us and that really helps. Probably a good example of this is, back in 1984, we ran a campaign to stop the aerial shooting of wolves in British Columbia . . . and I recruited Bo Derek for the sex and the celebrity. At the press conference, which was packed, a reporter from the *Vancouver Sun* said, 'What does Bo Derek know about wolves?' And I said, 'That is not the point. Have you just graduated from journalism school or something? I could have the best wolf biologist in the world here and I'd have an empty room. But the fact that she's our spokesperson means the place is packed and it will be the headline in your newspaper tomorrow. You're going to write it and there's not a damn thing you can do about it, is there?' They set the rules. We just play by their rules. (Interview, 21 January 2009)

News media have long been interested in celebrity; celebrity has long been a feature of politics; and celebrities have long advocated on behalf of the environment (Turner 2004; Marshall 2005; Brockington 2009). But in the last decades of the twentieth century and first years of the twenty-first, these connections have strengthened significantly via a convergence of factors: changes within news media, such as so-called 'tabloidization'; a growth in the publicity and promotional industries, including celebrity agents and entertainment marketing and public relations; and the 'mainstreaming' of the environment as a cause and a subsequent capacity for some parts of the environment movement to attract powerful celebrity allies. A study on Australian media and celebrity found that between 1977 and 1997 there was a dramatic increase in the number of stories devoted to celebrities in the daily press, with, for example, the number of celebrity stories more than doubling in the quality broadsheet, the *Sydney Morning Herald* (Turner et al. 2000: 19–23). The change was of a comparable magnitude to that occurring in other media forms, including women's magazines and television news bulletins, and was in close correlation to the overall growth in the Australian publicity and promotional industries. For David Marshall, this expansion of coverage has been accompanied by a 'naturalization and normalization of the close connection between the sources of information and journalistic practice; in other words, celebrity journalism is one of the key locations for the convergence of publicity, promotion and journalism in terms of the generated editorial content' (2005: 28). Celebrity is now clearly a part of the political realm, both in how we go about politics and how we understand it, and it will continue to be so (Gamson 1994: 192; Schlesinger 2006: 301).

Celebrity takes many forms, and to begin to understand the relationship between celebrity, news and environmental politics, we must first attempt a celebrity 'taxonomy' (Boykoff and Goodman 2009). We can start by identifying politicians, such as Al Gore; celebrity scientists, such as David Attenborough; celebrity activists, such as Zac Goldsmith; and activist celebrities, including the growing number of entertainers who are publicly associated with an environmental cause. Yet, even this rudimentary list shows the difficulties in any clear separation, as activists (Goldsmith) stand for parliament and former politicians (Gore) become activists, while entertainers become politicians or better known for their activism than their commercial product, as has occurred with Bob Geldof and Bono through their humanitarian work. We also should not dismiss the impact of the non-human celebrity, as the story of El Grande above shows. Knut, the polar bear cub from the Berlin Zoo, is another example. The May 2007 'Green Issue' of *Vanity Fair*, the magazine that uniquely combines celebrity with politics, depicted actor Leonardo di Caprio and Knut together on its US cover, but left di Caprio off for its German edition (Associated Press in Berlin 2007).

Representing a cause is now part of the entertainment celebrity job description. 'Who will dress you?' and 'Which cause will you represent?' are two questions commonly asked by agents when they sign on a new client (Lester 2010a). Indeed, an extensive US study of celebrity, activist websites and media presence found that 62.8 per cent of celebrities were engaged in advocacy and were, on average, active on 1.8 issues and involved with 1.8 groups (Thrall et al. 2008: 367). These figures increased markedly for celebrities listed on the 'Forbes 100' list, with ninety per cent involved in advocacy, participating on average in 4.16 issues and 3.45 groups. Environment was the fifth most common area in which celebrities were involved, below social welfare, health and children's welfare but well above partisan politics. There has also been a marked increase in the US in celebrity political donations and in the number of celebrities testifying before Congress (Thrall et al. 2008: 374).

Celebrity functions politically by carrying 'meaning in situations far beyond what might reasonably be seen to be their professional expertise and to audiences far exceeding those who might be supposed to be interested in the products they represent' (Turner et al. 2000: 164). Celebrity deployment is thus a tempting path for environmental pressure groups; a form of tradable commodity that used within certain circumstances and in combination with other tactics can potentially strengthen and mobilize existing support, alert new supporters to causes, and provide a conduit to policymakers. Nevertheless, it is also problematic in that its peculiar logics can impact on the internal structures and practices of social movements. Movements may choose leaders for their celebrity-style politics, fulfilling the needs of the media but not necessarily the needs of the membership (Gitlin 1980: 176), while movement leaders may take a back seat to celebrity supporters who, new to a group's values and practices, take over the roles of high-profile 'activists'. According to Meyer and Gamson, 'The story of social protest then becomes a celebrity story, and not one that includes politics, policy, or space for grass roots action' (1995: 187). Celebrities will also seek to be involved in causes in which they will have some kind of credibility or which will not harm their carefully managed identities, potentially creating a 'softening effect' on movement aims overall. As Meyer and Gamson write, 'Celebrities bring with them significant incentives to shift movement frames, and in particular to depoliticize or deradicalize movement claims.

Participation by celebrities then can speed the process of institutionalizing and domesticating dissent' (1995: 188).

Paul Watson's Sea Shepherd Society provides an interesting example of how celebrities can be deployed to further a group's aims, while their presence and symbolic power can also be contained in a way that such risks are minimized. Celebrities are associated with Sea Shepherd in several ways. They may be linked to the organization by name. For example, Sea Shepherd's Media and Arts Advisory Board includes actors Martin Sheen, Sean Penn, Rutger Hauer, Brigitte Bardot and Linda Blair, names that can direct web and other traffic towards the organization. They may also become the focus of mediated events, as with US actress Daryl Hannah, who joined Watson in 2009 'using her celebrity to raise awareness'.

From a celebrity and promotional industry perspective, Watson's cause – saving whales and other marine creatures – would be considered generally safe and an opportunity for further promotion by the entertainment industry. His confrontational

Figure 6.3   Paul Watson and Daryl Hannah in the news (courtesy of The Mercury, Hobart)

actions and non-compromising speech, however, would be less appealing from a celebrity management perspective. Thus, only certain types of celebrity identities will be safe within the Sea Shepherd cause; the action persona (Penn, Sheen), and the committed animal activist (Bardot, Hannah), to name two. Watson's use of celebrities is also measured. Appointments to his Arts and Media Board keep celebrities actively visible, while also containing their power within the frame of the entertainment industry. This allows Watson to capitalize on both the increasing celebrity presence within contemporary news media and the increasing pressure on celebrities from the promotional industries to engage in (the right kind of) political activity, without experiencing the potential 'softening effect' of celebrity. Nevertheless, Watson will also encourage supporters to take on political leadership roles when the occasion warrants and under certain conditions, as this quote shows:

> For instance, I write speeches for Pierce Brosnan. I did the Global Green one, and he calls me up and says the *LA Times* want to print the speech. He said, 'I had to tell them you wrote it.' And I said, 'Well, you shouldn't have done that. They're not going to print it now. The speech coming from you is a news item. Coming from me, it's not.' That's just the reality of it. (Interview, 21 January 2009)

However, it is still uncertain how, and indeed if, celebrity involvement with a group, cause or issue translates into news coverage and political engagement. While there was a dramatic rise in media coverage of celebrity and climate change in 2005 and 2006, Boykoff and Goodman remain uncertain if overall coverage of the environmental issue was boosted by its celebrity association, or vice versa (2009). The US celebrity website study finds no significant evidence of a connection between celebrity involvement with an environmental group or cause and increased news coverage; its authors argue that increased celebrity stories about an issue simply follow increased interest in that issue overall, and that even the power of celebrity is unable to break through the traditional blockages to news access for many advocacy groups (Thrall et al. 2008). Audience research also remains undecided: a

UK-based study found little evidence that an interest in celebrity will lead people to a fuller engagement with the news (Couldry et al. 2007: 187), but a survey of Steve Irwin fans found that television news was the way most people heard about the Australian 'wildlife warrior's' death. They then turned to internet-based news for further information, as well as to interpersonal communication and his organization's website, where donations increased dramatically (Brown 2010). Irwin's fans actively followed the news.

Returning briefly to Tasmania provides some insight into how the interconnection of news, celebrities and environmental politics may be evolving. Celebrities have been consistently present over the forty years of the conflict, although the roles played by various types of celebrity within the media have changed significantly over that period. For example, well-known figures in the 1960s–80s who were allowed to 'speak' politically within the news media were the mountain climbers, national parks advocates, scientists, business leaders and politicians who had long-standing interest or expertise in the area. Their right to voice an opinion and their role as a source was only questioned by journalists when they chose to stress their celebrity status over their expertise, as did UK television ecologist David Bellamy when he travelled to Tasmania in late 1982 from the UK to participate in the Franklin Blockade action. On arrival, he declared that he was there to use his celebrity to attract international attention to the cause, creating a flurry of negative media attention (Lester 2007: 132). While entertainers, such as soap stars and singers, also participated in the action, they generally appeared in the media visually, pictured leading protests or being arrested. Twenty years later, such a division no longer exists, with actors, singers and authors with no previous interest or expertise in an issue appearing within news coverage as political sources, even prompting debate about the issues themselves. Their right to participate in the conflict is not questioned, while the content of their statements is exposed to scrutiny in the same terms as it is with other political actors. In the Tasmanian context, this has exposed them to harsh public criticism, which predictably causes concern for their agents and others involved in promoting them as entertainers to as wide an audience as possible. In turn, environmental groups are careful in the way they use different types of celebrity. Young stars of the TV soap *Neighbours*, for example, have been used to lead but not speak at demonstrations, while more well-known and powerful actors will be given 'speaking roles' (Lester 2010a). Overall, celebrity remains a highly visible part of the movement's strategy for news access and public communication within the Tasmanian conflict, but the strengths and weaknesses of celebrity participation is such that it is carefully deployed.

Clearly, more work is needed to understand the complexities of connections and flows between celebrity, political engagement and news. Al Gore's *An Inconvenient Truth* is widely credited with the increase in public attention to climate change from 2005–6. Yet, at work within and around Gore and the public and political reach of his film was Gore's own political credibility and networks, his celebrity-style personification of the issue, the international entertainment industry promoting the film, and the massive quantity and transnational flow of news about the film and its political consequences. Gore and his film were the subject of fierce public debate about the validity and impact of such an intervention into the climate change issue, much of which reflects broader concerns about the celebritization and spectacularization of politics. On the one hand, celebrities can breach the science/media divide, both humanizing environmental science and symbolizing widespread concern and calls for action (Boykoff and Goodman 2009: 404). On the other, they are something to greet with more caution; in seeking 'conspicuous redemption', they may be creating yet another 'palliative balm to soothe our collective consciousness, embedded still in largely capitalist and modernist frameworks' (Boykoff and Goodman 2009: 404).

Another expressed anxiety concerns the capacity of audiences to decode the celebritized, spectacular images carried by celebrity into the political arena, and to see beyond the simplified symbolic associations celebrities and their political promoters seek to invoke. For Dan Brockington, this is of particular relevance within the muddied waters of environmental NGO status and might, which allows celebrity to empower some forms of land conservation at the expense of social justice measures, such as encouraging the continuation of indigenous or other traditional land use practices. 'There can be a dark underbelly to the work of conservation that is rarely discussed in public, and, in celebrity conservation, all the glitz and razzmatazz, the bright lights and glamour, will just obscure the misfortunes all the more' (Brockington 2009: 22). Still others are concerned by the capacity of celebrity, and NGO exploitation of that capacity, to actually shift the arena of public debate away from the shared space of news media to the splintered, partisan world of celebrity and activist websites. About half the advocacy groups surveyed by Thrall and his colleagues (2008) use the entertainment medium to push their messages: they stage concerts and arrange for celebrities to arrive at awards ceremonies in hybrid vehicles. They also use celebrities to draw potential supporters to their websites, such as with the coalition between the Natural Resources Defense Council and the rock group Green Day. Three short videos on the NRDC website, which show Green Day band members talking about the importance of protecting the environment, were viewed a total of 622,338 times less than a year after being posted on the web (2008: 379). Thrall et al. argue that the consequences of such a shift challenge the American political system; despite the imperfections of the traditional mass media news system, it does present a range of information and views for public debate (Thrall et al. 2008: 383).

Here, then, the symbolic power of challenger groups to intervene in environmental politics is approached warily; the interconnections and fluidity of the contemporary media landscape are such that celebrity is accused of forming a symbolic bridge over which the news bastion is invaded and eventually taken by the promotional and entertainment industries. However, when analysed within broader contexts, celebrity emerges as part of an integrated media strategy, one that is still attuned to news media entry. Access to the news remains a primary ambition of activist groups and this, in turn, ensures its continuing relevance and therefore power. As such – and just as we saw in relation to protest – it is still too early to dismiss news as a central forum for and player in environmental politics, and not least for its potential to engage publics in their environmental futures, and those of others.

7

Environment and Engagement

The two most popular Causes on Facebook in June 2009:

Stop Global Warming (3,007,094 members – $33,178 donated)
Save Water, Drink Beer (973,773 members – $115 donated)

It all means nothing if nobody cares. Environmentalists may organize protests that achieve massive media presence or circulate images with startling symbolic messages at their core; journalists may overcome professional practices that prevent environmental issues from being considered within news coverage beyond a short-term focus on events or conflict, or from being sustained or debated in depth; scientists may disguise or hide disputes that can be represented by journalists and 'sceptics' or 'deniers' as evidence of 'bad' science rather than of 'uncertain' science, and learn to speak the language of journalism; industry, government and other powerful sources may expand their media relations efforts and increase resourcing to counter challenges from environmental groups; ordinary people may achieve access to the news not only to tell occasional and emotional stories of loss, or of fear, but to become rational voices, credible sources, within mediated environmental debate. But it all means nothing if nobody cares.

And acts. To varying degrees and in differing ways, media invite their audiences, their readers and viewers, to respond. It may be an invitation to respond emotionally; to feel outrage, sadness, fear, shame or – perhaps – satisfied, complacent, helpless, empowered. Some responses may be accompanied by a desire and capacity to act. What might be done? What action can be taken? Who should I contact? Sometimes, the invitation itself may be more direct; participate in a poll, register a vote, donate money, call this number, turn out the lights. Numerous studies have warned of the difficulties in establishing clear connections between media consumption and public participation, and of the dangers of assuming a shared or sustained orientation towards public affairs (Couldry et al. 2007). Nevertheless, how news not only informs but engages its audiences is an increasingly important question for media research because embedded within it are broader debates about citizenship and democracy, about the formation of publics and a strengthened civil society, and about how people may be politically, socially and environmentally engaged in the future with its rapidly changing and uncertain media landscape.

Three possibilities emerge above in terms of type and degree of engagement that may be media related: interest in an issue, affect for an issue and participation in activities connected to an issue. Interest is more than fleeting attention but could also imply concern, one that is shared with others. Affect suggests an emotional involvement, a stronger reaction, even commitment, to the concerns. Participation is an active response to these other forms of engagement, and brings to the fore the shared nature of the concerns and the act of 'joining'. Participation, as Peter Dahlgren reminds us in a political context, must be 'more than simply a feeling one has, it involves some "activity"', and without such activity, engagement itself will at some point dissipate (2009: 81).

It is this – participation – that strengthens our claim to citizenship, not simply having an interest or emotional response to an issue. As Dahlgren writes: 'Following the news daily only makes one a potentially better citizen' (2009: 81).

We live in highly mediated societies, and much of our civic knowledge derives from the media. In a sense, the media bear some responsibility for our political involvement: good journalism must at some point engage us in the world it presents to us. Yet we as citizens also have a democratic responsibility to become engaged and to participate. (Dahlgren 2009: 81)

Within the context of environmental risk, concerns and debates, the idea of the active citizen is a compelling one because it is here – with individuals acting together for a common good – that the possibility emerges of a shared environmentally secure future. Media roles and responsibilities in animating such civic activity raise equally compelling questions. A number of studies have connected media coverage of global warming, for example, with increased awareness of the issue among publics (see Castells 2009: 315–21), but we need to also ask what role do media play in influencing decision makers – both personal and political – to work towards a common goal of environmental sustainability. Where does responsibility lie for encouraging such environmental citizenship? With individuals? With media? With media sources?

And within which boundaries are these roles and responsibilities located? Local? National? Global? Or are the parameters defined less by geography and more by values and ethics? News media, both 'old' and 'new', continually face the decision on how to manage the permeability of these boundaries; the flow of information and symbolic content from place to place, the capacity of this content to influence and engage audiences, the need to create hierarchies and privileges. This is not new – even the earliest newspapers were required to rank information depending on its geographical and political or social source – but the speed of the information flow, the amount of content available, and the quantity and variety of outlets for publication and broadcast are unprecedented. Moreover, these boundaries are not only permeable but transforming. This change, according to Manuel Castells, is three-dimensional: we now live in a space that is both global and local in that what happens globally depends on what we do locally; the fast-paced time of our daily lives contrasts ever more greatly with the 'glacial time' of our relationship with the environment; and our boundaries, our social organization, must now be conceived in terms of the future – of 'intergenerational solidarity' – as well as the past and the present (2009: 337–8).

We therefore need to remain closely attuned to change and difference if we want to better understand mediated communication about the environment and its capacity and/or will to encourage environmental citizenship. We know, for example, that UK television news stories are more likely to focus on the inevitability of suffering and conflict, compared to Swedish news reports, which invariably focus on human agency (Robertson 2010: 91–2). Alexa Robertson found this to be the case in the reporting of the 2004 Boxing Day tsunami. Swedish reporting did not focus on Acts of God or even acts of nature, as UK news did – here 'suffering was not inevitable and always had human agents. At times it seemed as though the Swedish foreign minister was personally responsible for the flood' (Robertson 2010: 92).

The scale of environmental conflicts and crises now found in local, national and global debate and policy, and the capacity of individuals and publics to both become victims of environmental degradation and contribute to environmental risk and solutions, are such that it is imperative we continue to ask what it is that media do to engage their audiences across a range of contexts. We can begin to do this by questioning how environmental images, words and symbols carried by the news media potentially connect with the everyday lives of people, and thus how ordinary people – as well as policy and decision makers – might find a willingness and capacity to respond and act. But we can also ask what media and those around them could do better. These are the tasks of this final chapter.

Engaging citizens

To consider the first question – what it is that media do to engage their audiences – I want to return in some detail to the six-country sample of television news introduced in Chapter One, and specifically to ask how news visuals may have contributed to the constitution of climate change as a global issue. Here, a more complex picture emerges of how climate change is 'made visible' and 'ecological images and symbols' can, potentially, 'generate pressure for action' (Beck 2009: 86). Such an analysis draws together many of the concerns raised throughout this book and helps illuminate the connection between the work of news media, media sources and ideas of citizenship, both in terms of our care for local communities and places, but also to our often solely mediated connections to distant peoples and environments – perhaps the emergent cosmopolitanism suggested by Ulrich Beck (see Lester and Cottle 2009 for further discussion).

We know that visual symbols can command public attention in environmental politics, and spectacular images can help legitimize political challenges and mobilize support. We know also that images of the environment found within the news often come with historically long and culturally deep resonances, and so too can they contribute to our sense of self, identity and place in the world (Macnaghten and Urry 1998: 52; Franklin et al. 2000: 26; Cottle 2006: 130–7). Recent research also indicates that television visuals can play an important role in the development of global environmental awareness and contribute to a sense of ecological citizenship and associated rights and responsibilities (Urry 1999, 2000; Szerszynski and Toogood 2000; Szerszynski and Urry 2002, 2006). Through this research, Szerszynski highlights the tension that exists within the concept of environmental citizenship, between dwelling in a local place with the moral rights and responsibilities that entails, and developing a sense of global responsibility, which relies in part on absenting oneself from a particular place via 'a transformation of vision, one that relies on an imaginative removal of the self from immediate everyday engagement in the world' (2006: 75). Emphasizing the importance of the visual in the practice of citizenship, Szerszynski notes that to be an environmental citizen, 'is to have one's perceptions and actions in a local context transformed by an awareness of that locality's connections with and nesting within a wider, ultimately global context' (2006: 75).

Here, images of 'banal globalism' can play their part. These almost unnoticed symbols of globalism that now routinely feature across televisual images and narratives help to create a 'sensibility to the cosmopolitan rights and duties of being a "global citizen"' (Szerszynski et al. 2000: 99). Three particularly significant categories of media images provide, argue Szerszynski et al., 'unremarked-upon' global context for various kinds of action:

the globe, which suggests we all belong to the same planet; environments, which symbolize wider threats and risks; and people, including celebrities, who are made to stand and speak for the human race (2000: 103–5). These images propose 'possible relations to other people and the Earth as a whole, and such new sets of relations can carry powerful feelings of helplessness or responsibility, distance or engagement' (2000: 106).

The six-country study found that within news on climate change, symbolic and spectacular visuals are deployed in more than half of all stories, notably more than in the coverage of other global crises, including those connected to terrorism or refugees. (Symbolic visuals were identified as those visuals that represent something larger or broader than the image itself, beyond the literal – for example, visuals of black smoke pouring out of factories in a news item about industrial air pollution; and spectacular visuals as those that seemingly invite responses of awe or dread – for example, slow panning shots of pristine wilderness and shots that dwell on natural landscapes, or alternatively visuals focusing on the destructive force of extreme weather events.) Such images can play a prominent part in 'bringing home' the threat and reality of global climate change. For example, stand-alone symbolic images and spectacular filmic flows that encourage an affective response range across scenes of sunsets over an ice-filled sea to the sunrise over a tiny Pacific island, from trees bent in hurricane-force winds to billowing smoke sourced to an ugly industrial landscape. Such images invite viewers to recognize and possibly respond to the rise and risks of climate change – whether at local, national and/or global levels.

As noted in the previous chapter, depictions of the globe in the context of news on climate change have now become commonplace in the media, as they have in the iconography of news journalism more generally. The stock of global imagery is also deployed to call attention to the specificity of local places threatened by climate change. Reports in a series on the UK's Channel 5, dubbed 'Disappearing World', begin for example with a graphic, referencing a satellite image showing continents and oceans, before highlighting the threatened locality in question. This serves both to locate the subject of the story, and to draw the viewer's attention to the universality and globality of the crisis one local community faces, which is revealed via the spectacular visuals that follow. Likewise, maps are not only static representations of far away threatened places that depict 'locations less as inhabited places and as decontextualized formations, distant and irrelevant to Western spectators' (Chouliaraki 2006: 101), but can also be integrated into the 'symbolic fabric' of threatened lives and possible solutions in a highly localized way. In the climate change sample, for example, maps appear on the walls of victim's homes alongside photographs of family members, or behind the desks of scientists, or in the hands of local officials out in the field. Close-ups of fingers pointing to features on these maps not only further localize the problem, but also humanize it.

Television visuals are often grounded in a particular place and lives, and in so doing private loss is revealed, the threat becomes a domestic one, and viewers in their own homes are invited to care. This is repeated time and again through the climate change sample, using a variety of visual devices. For example, stories on disappearing glaciers in China and Nepal use establishing mid-shots of domestic streetscapes with residents going about their business before panning up or zooming out to reveal distant mountains and rocky surfaces exposed by retreating ice. This flow between the domestic and a threatened environment reinforces the connection between people's lives and nature. In a variant, the camera pans from a domestic street scene in the UK to rest on the industrial landscape behind that spews smoke into an already darkened sky. Here, the connection is visually reinforced further, identifying the source of the threat. Clearer still are the scenes of private domesticity within the threatened landscape, such as in stories about coastal damage in Alaska and the UK. Families are shown preparing meals in the homes that the stories have already established as threatened. The stories cut from within the home, to distant exterior shots to reinforce the imminent risk, to back inside with the victims. A particularly powerful and often repeated variant shows people packing up belongings getting ready to leave their homes.

Figure 7.1   *Disappearing World,* Five News, Channel 5 UK

Cultural resonances that are embedded in the past and are reliant on shared or imagined memories are also repeatedly called upon to establish the magnitude of crisis and loss, and invite the viewer to care. Personal photographs of victims' family members stress the longevity and right to belong to a place (see Figures 7.1 and 7.2), as are establishing shots of cemeteries, ruined schools and garden debris. The camera repeatedly dwells upon the elderly and children, 'being' in the threatened environment. Children playing in snow on a melting Chinese glacier, women praying in a Nepalese temple; these are activities that translate visually across to distant viewers' cultural memories and lived experiences and deploy nostalgia as a device to encourage a sense of impending loss for not only an environment but also national cultures and pastimes (Featherstone 1993).

Moving away from a focus on a specific place and into the realm of symbolic 'environments', there are stocks of certain key visuals found to be commonly associated with climate change reporting, and these can be categorized into two main categories of *causes* and *impacts*. Cause images in the context of climate change reporting comprise billowing smokestacks, coal-fired power stations and traffic on freeways. As noted in the previous chapter, here the meaning for most Western viewers is clear and does not call upon complex cultural connections. The second set of visuals operates in a less straightforward fashion. These *impact* visuals can be split into *natural* and *human* impacts. The *natural impact* visuals are disconnected from humanity: the dripping glacier, the collapsing edge of an ice shelf, bared mountain rocks, the racing mountain stream, the lone polar bear pulling itself onto a small piece of ice. The *human impact* visuals, in contrast, are symbolically associated with individual and communal suffering and loss: suburban palm trees bent almost to the ground by wind, violent waves crashing over concrete retaining walls, the debris-strewn post-storm coastline, victims wading through flooded streets. When used in stories with a central focus on climate change, these images, often unanchored by explanatory words (Barthes 1977: 38–41), rely on the viewer to draw connections between storm events and global warming. These three sets of images – *cause*, and natural and human *impact* visuals – appear regularly together and in various combinations and sequences in climate change stories.

Importantly, we need to be aware that it is not just the presence and arrangement of visuals nor the referencing of extreme weather events within a climate change story that invite viewer response, but also how the flow of images and symbols within these and other stories now deploy similar 'stock' visuals. Here, visual intertextuality is increasingly likely to be at work, with similar images potentially relaying (Barthes 1977: 41) signs of climate change within, for example, news reporting of hurricanes or bushfires. While scientific and political discourse may have once been largely silent on any connection between climate change and extreme weather events within standard news reporting of disasters, the deployment of extreme weather visuals in climate change stories encourages the implicit link for the viewer. When this visual relay becomes so evident as to call into question the integrity of the news story frame, scientific and political news sources are then called upon, in a more discursive form of news entry, to either acknowledge or dispel the connection, details of which will be discussed below. Images of the globe, for example, are common in both climate change reporting as well as in disaster reporting, with dramatic satellite pictures tracking the course of hurricanes and disappearing ice-sheets, deforestation and forest fires – such parallel use of visual sequences and scenes can only encourage

Figure 7.2 *Disappearing World*, Five News, Channel 5 UK

visual relay and the possible connection with climate change in the foreseeable future.

'Human impact' visuals that cross between these two subject areas include families leaving their homes, victims inspecting debris-strewn waterways, individuals battling gale force winds. These 'impact' visuals can work with the 'cause' visuals to mutually reinforce a global sense of responsibility not only at the level of shared humanity, but – for the Western viewer – of actually being responsible for the problem, causing the crisis itself. This invocation is often further underlined by the complex calls for compassion and empathy that can be embedded within disaster reporting (Chouliaraki 2006) and contrasted with the politicized and conflictual space occupied by the climate change issue. As we have seen, journalistic norms and practices might usually prevent such direct invitations to respond and act within reporting on such a contested issue, but less so when framed in the depoliticized terms of humanitarian emergency. Of course, when the hurricanes are threatening the most powerful industrial nation and viewers witness the suffering of Westerners, the invitation is made even more strongly, reminding viewers that they may one day suffer through such environmental disaster themselves (Lindahl Elliot 2006: 233–4).

Although moving scenes and images of nature, people and places under threat from climate change may well prove essential for the formation of public awareness and growing concerns, spectacle remains insufficient as a basis for processes of mobilization and political responses. As Simon Cottle has argued, such scenes cannot substitute for the necessary public elaboration and engagement of contending environmental perspectives and discourses (2000: 43). How Ulrich Beck's 'relations of definition' or the strategic play of different views and voices, identities and interests enter the news domain also performs a crucial role in television news' communication of climate change. And here issues of trust can become critical, with viewers seeking to gauge the credibility and legitimacy of experts, spokespeople and other claims makers and assessing their right to speak on behalf of others. As Macnaghten and Urry note, 'issues of trust are central to whether or not people believe media stories about environmental matters, and to the extent to which they will be likely to identify with, or participate in, officially defined environmental initiatives' (1998: 99–100).

In the television news sample, just as ordinary people are usually visualized as victims, or Beck's 'voices of the side effects', shown within domestic settings or overcoming/succumbing to the impacts of climate change, political and scientific sources – the experts, consultants and spokespeople – have a similarly restricted repertoire of visual backdrops and locales in which to be interviewed or contextualized through establishing sequences. These, however, generally provide the source with a sense of purpose, duty, engagement and credibility. Scientists, for example, are usually shown either at work in the field, which is invariably a harsh and challenging environment threatened by the effects of climate change, or at their desk with screens, files and work colleagues in the background (see Figure 7.3). Scientists in these settings do more than give information and opinions to the viewer. Firstly, they 'bear witness' of the crisis for the public, if not with their own eyes then through the screen or reports on their desks. But, secondly, they also act. They measure glaciers and peer into the mouths of polar bears. They study maps and aerial photographs, and work in bustling offices and laboratories, where they are too busy engaging with the crisis to be interviewed anywhere other than at their desk. This visual engagement with scientific sources in television news carries with it a public call to trust. This is reinforced by the fact that, in the longer reportage stories in the sample, journalists are often positioned on camera engaging closely with their scientific sources. They discuss maps and historical photographs, and together locate landscape features. In this way, the credibility of the journalist as climate change 'expert' is also being visually reinforced, while also diminishing any sense of contestation or conflict surrounding the source.

Politicians in the sample are usually shown addressing a crowd, in a studio interview or, as with the UK prime minister on the eve of his major speech on climate change, inspecting the effects or technological products of climate change, such as solar panels. Politicians are thus visually afforded a similar capacity as scientists to engage with both the problem of and the solution to climate change. Political dress, specifically the suit jacket, it appears, is a barrier to full engagement with the environment – as politicians have found it to be when dealing hands on with any social problem in front of cameras – and climate change news is certainly not immune to the visual rolling-up-the-sleeves metaphor. The focus is on the individual's capacity to be both one of us and to lead us through the crisis. The popular cut-away shot to press photographers at the photo op, media conference or public address serves in this context to reinforce the centrality of the individual to the issue.

In contrast to politicians and scientists, climate change activists

Figure 7.3 *Climate change science,* Today in Africa, SABC Africa

and NGO spokespeople are regularly interviewed and shown standing outside. They are in the landscape, but statically. They stand against a backdrop of 'nature', if only a tree or park, but do not engage with it in any way. Moreover, they are invariably firmly planted in a single locale. For local activists – for example, the spokesperson for the local coastal action group – this makes sense. Their concerns, discursively presented via interview, are supported by the visual backdrop of a specific threatened place. This does not make sense, however, when the interviewee represents a major international NGO, such as Greenpeace. Here, spokespeople of these transnational advocacy movements are rarely associated with possible visual indicators of a global sensibility and significance when accessed in such news formats as, for example, the studio-based interview or across from a busy office. Rather, they are grounded in a single place, thus crudely at best visualizing their global conception of environmental concerns, transnational actions and politics aimed as problem-solving capacity.

This visual distancing of challenger groups and NGOs from the core of political cooperation and possible solution to the global crisis is reinforced by a repeated sequence shown in climate change television news. Here, the nation state and its formal government are granted visual supremacy in international efforts to solve the global crisis. The news events are formal international gatherings but the camera typically rests on a table sign, bearing the name of 'its' nation, before zooming out to show dozens more such signs and their national representatives. Another story has the camera panning from a single flag across dozens of others, to finally rest on a speaker addressing a large formal meeting. These stories begin by establishing climate change as a problem through the utilization of spectacular visuals of smokestacks, blocked freeways and/or extreme weather events, and thus position and visualize the multinational gathering and 'the nation' as the key contributor to solving the global crisis. Of course, this visual primacy provided to the nation state in finding a solution to climate change may be nothing more than a symptom of a still emerging global culture (Featherstone 1993) and the very limited repertoire of symbols and images by which television news is able to portray global cooperation. However, the sample suggests that television news carries an ongoing visual commitment to the nation state and/or has not yet found the necessary repertoire to adequately visualize Beck's explosion of boundaries and political agendas, and birth of global publics (2006: 6, 35–6).

Thus, in these ways, the mediated politics of climate change becomes conditioned by twin visual rhetorics, each capable of working independently as well as in powerful combination, to variously help mobilize or mute appeals to environmental citizenship. The visual rhetorics are complexly involved in the constitution and mobilization of climate change as a global issue and can encourage ecological citizenship and even, possibly, lend sustenance to Beck's ideas concerning a discerned and emergent cosmopolitan outlook. But how this symbolic politics of the media becomes visualized in practice and played out on the news stage also exhibits complexities and contradictions, and these too often continue to detract from news media's potential to generate pressure for action.

Engaging media

For the Civil Rights movement in the mid-twentieth century United States, the key to mobilizing support from afar was drama. As Jeffrey Alexander writes, these activists 'tried as hard as they could to ensure that the drama would be presented to the surrounding civil audience in a manner that would evoke sympathy, generate identification, and extend solidarity' (2006: 305).

> How could white northern civil society be there, in the South, yet not be there at the same time? When its physical presence was barely tangible, how could its moral presence be strongly felt? How could its representatives be compelled to intervene in a society toward which they had earlier evinced so little interest and on which they had exercised so little control? This could happen only through a process of emotional identification and symbolic extension ... Tragic drama

excites in the audience pity and terror, and sympathy for the protagonist's plight. The progression of protagonist and antagonist can eventually allow catharsis, an emotional working through that affirms not only the existence but the force of higher moral law. The Civil Rights movement was not scripted: it was a social movement, not a text. Nonetheless, the contingent, open-ended nature of its conflicts were symbolically mediated and textually informed. Life imitates art as much as art imitates life. (Alexander 2006: 306)

Half a century later, our concern is a different movement, a different conflict, and a stage of vastly different scale. We are confronted with unnerving variations on the 'tragic drama' of movement politics, of political conflict. What happens when antagonists cannot be clearly identified or, as Beck describes it, 'organized irresponsibility' becomes a key feature of the drama? What happens if the protagonists are the leaders of a global movement speaking politically on behalf of victims who are far away and, in their billions, largely voiceless? Yet an important similarity remains: the need of those involved in the political drama to 'evoke sympathy, generate identification and extend solidarity'. News media have survived to date as central to fulfilling this need; for most members of civil society, according to Alexander, news is the only source of first-hand experience 'they will ever have about their fellow citizens, about their motives for acting the way they do, the kinds of relationships they form, and the nature of the institutions they might potentially create' (2006: 80). This raises more concerns. What happens if news media – a key conduit between environmental risk, the public and potential solutions – become so inured or antagonistic towards political drama that the actors, scripts and props are often, but not uniformly, not equally, exposed? What happens if news media, knowing there can be no final act, stop covering the drama? And what happens if the main actors in the drama, faced with continuing inconsistencies and inequalities, move to a different stage?

This book has considered these possibilities from a range of historical and contemporary viewpoints. It has stressed the complexities, contingencies and contradictions that are evident within the relationship between news media and conflicts about the environment. It has attempted to provide a set of tools for identifying and understanding specific features and dynamics of the relationship; what it is that news media and those around news media do and how this may affect our awareness of environmental issues and concerns and our capacity to act to secure our environmental futures. To conclude, this final section returns to the four interconnected points made in Chapter One that provided a broad framework from which to consider the relationship between media and environment. They also provide a framework for asking how the relationship might be strengthened and, most importantly, sustained.

The first was that we need to look deeply at news media coverage, directly but also behind the texts to the activities of the journalists and sources, and to the specifics of the ways in which news is created and circulated. News texts are important. They provide insight into the world around us; into events, issues and people; into public concerns about shared futures. Analyses of news texts can usefully draw our attention to privileged access or exclusion within the news, and as we saw in Chapter Three in relation to climate change coverage, this can have serious implications for the quality of information that circulates within the public sphere. Such analyses can also suggest how such coverage emerges into the news arena: the socially open nature of news exposes it, for example, to ideological predispositions within a newsroom or to the professional practices of journalists when faced with a complex issue. Words, quotes, sources, position, images, length, headlines, combine to form news texts that join with other news texts to create coverage that may or may not work powerfully to impact on public debate and decision making.

But looking at news texts can only take us so far. Many factors drive journalists in their daily work and some will vary when the issue being covered is the environment. Complexities presented by scientific jargon, perceptions within newsrooms of environmental journalists as activists, the scope of risk and possible solutions; these are some of the differences that have been identified and impact on environmental news. As Chapter

Four highlighted, the practices of journalists must also be viewed alongside the activities of those around them. Over the last two decades, the massive increase in the size and sophistication of the public relations and promotional industries have combined with parallel commercial and resourcing pressures on traditional journalism to leave news media increasingly vulnerable. The impact of these twin dynamics on news about the environment has remained hidden for too long. Just as news media have been willing to expose the 'theatre' of environmental protest to their readers and viewers for decades, they must now be willing to expose the activities of their powerful sources for scrutiny. There is evidence that this is occurring more frequently – investigations into the PR and lobbying work of the fossil fuel industries in the US and Australia in particular have exposed how much effort is concentrated not only on influencing political decision makers, but also on influencing news media content. Trust in news media is less likely to be destroyed by such revelations than a continuing lack of transparency about the sources and contexts of environmental coverage.

By going behind the scenes of news production, the struggle over media power becomes clearer, and two key features are revealed: the first is that news media will work to maintain control of the news agenda against some actors in environmental debate; it will, for example, only rarely circulate powerful symbols generated by the environment movement, only rarely allow ordinary people access beyond a symbolic role of victim or concerned citizen. Yet, news media too readily hand the power to shape the news agenda to other political actors, and do so in such a way that the transaction is not revealed. The second is that once we look at what sources do in and around the news, we see that news remains a key site of struggle, of conflict. The use of movement websites and protest activity outlined in Chapter Five shows that – for all its flaws, inequities and inconsistencies – news remains the 'main game' in much environmental politics. How news will be delivered in the future may still be unclear, but environmental source activity indicates that news continues to have an important role in the conflicts and debates about environmental futures.

The second point also highlighted the need to look beyond media's more discursive, word-based content, but in this case we should ask how symbols and images work to influence and shape environmental knowledge. Symbols and spectacular images clearly play a central role in environmental politics. Again, this is evident in the effort NGOs such as Greenpeace have put into their production and circulation, and more recently in the attempts by industry, governments and commercial interests to appropriate and harness their power. But we also need to be aware that images and symbols circulating via news media do not function in precisely the same way as those circulating in other forums such as advertising. Within television news coverage of climate change, symbolic and spectacular images may be deployed more commonly than in coverage of other global crises, as we saw in the previous section, but we can also witness examples of news media restricting the circulation of powerful symbols if they have been generated or promoted by the environment movement, such as in the case of the death of El Grande.

Further complexities emerge when we look to recent trends within news media, including an increasing reliance on visuals produced and supplied from outside the newsroom. Few news organizations will be willing or able to resource editorial or even freelance staff to cover anti-whaling activities in Antarctic waters, and any footage they do produce is likely to be of poorer quality than that produced by the Animal Planet crew aboard the Sea Shepherd Society's ship, the *Steve Irwin*, which is circulated to television networks around the world within hours, if not minutes, of any dramatic event. As Chapter Five asked, are the demands of news such that the use of such movement-provided footage can only be justified if the events depicted are violent or extreme? But if news media continue their reluctance to use such footage while providing fewer resources to covering such events, this may restrict even further the opportunity for the political challengers to have their voices heard within public debate.

As noted in Chapter Six, we know that a heavy reliance on spectacular images and symbols can be counterproductive in the long-term. Over-use can lead to 'green fatigue', where audiences become inured to embedded calls for empathy or action. Or if they are too powerful, they may prompt only a sense of hopelessness, a sense that it is too late. Yet, within the context of news, images can maintain a power that more than a century of newspaper photography and half a century of television news bulletins have not disproven. And when images of violence, devastation or protest are now downloaded from YouTube or MySpace and republished in a newspaper or rebroadcast on the news, they gain a new power that can shift political debate and move people to act. Too often, we consider news and social networking as an either/or proposition. The circulation of powerful environmental symbols and images will, in the future, evidently rely on both.

The third related point suggested we should identify connections across stories, places and histories if we are to begin to understand how news media work within environmental debate to potentially engage publics in the environment as an issue and crisis. We share only some histories and only some decision-making bodies across national borders, yet the nature of environmental risk is such that it demands we find shared understandings of what we mean by risk, and what we agree is of value. News media play a central role in this through their capacity to manage information across a range of geographical and political contexts; local, national, transnational and, sometimes, global. Research is beginning to emerge that tackles the question of how media in different countries and contexts may not only inform but engage their audiences. To date, engagement with either broader politics or humanitarian emergencies have tended to be the focus of such work. While both are relevant to environmental issues and conflicts, we need to take care in presuming total applicability.

We need to know how environmental news works in different contexts. Without understanding the way in which risk is framed to publics in poorer, developing countries as opposed to their richer counterparts, or the political, organizational and professional dynamics behind that framing, we are not well equipped to negotiate solutions. But we also need to stay attuned to change that is occurring within and around news media on a regional level. Environmental conflict is often fought locally, and it is from here that solutions will inevitably emerge. Locally and nationally based environmental issues – from forestry, to water use, to nuclear power – have been able to piggyback on climate change to increase their presence in news agendas. The opposite is also true. Climate change has undoubtedly piggybacked on the conflict over Tasmania's forests to increase its presence in local media and debate. These mediated flows are important; as we saw in Chapter Five, national or international interest in a local environmental issue can mobilize support from afar, generating pressure and sometimes even prompting political action. Thus, we need to understand not only what media do in different places but, importantly, their role in the flow of political and environmental information between these places.

The fourth and final point made in Chapter One was that 'the environment' that is the subject of mediated public debate is constructed through complex processes of knowledge transfer, reflexive interactions, meaning making and symbolic interplay, where conflict, power and emotions are also engaged, and we need to become highly attuned to these processes and 'pulls' if we are to better understand media roles in environmental debate. Experience tells us that news media interest in environmental issues will wane. It will slowly fall away – it did so in the early 1970s and again after a peak in the late 1980s. Individuals and groups with environmental messages will struggle to access the news; journalists interested in environmental issues and debate will struggle for space and credibility. Yet many things have changed since 1989, among them the growth of the internet and the emergence of climate change as a global crisis.

On 7 December 2009, fifty-six major newspapers around the world, in forty-five countries and twenty languages, published the same editorial urging politicians and negotiators gathered in Copenhagen for the United Nations Climate Change Conference to agree on a deal to cut greenhouse emissions (Guardian 2009). The editorial concluded in this way: 'If we, with such different national and political perspectives, can agree on what must be done then surely our leaders can too.' The outcome of the Copenhagen talks may have been weak and inconclusive, but the roles and responsibilities adopted by these fifty-six newspapers in relation to the environment were remarkably clear. We should neither expect nor want media to fully agree on what is important. We will never all value the environment equally, and news coverage needs to continue to reflect these contending interests and debates. Nevertheless, while agreement among news media is neither necessary nor desirable, we do require their sustained interest in the environment.

News media do matter. That environmental reporters are increasingly the target of harassment and threats indicates that governments, industry and others care about what news media publish and broadcast about the environment. Reporters Without Borders claim that fifteen per cent of the cases that the group monitors worldwide are now linked to the environment, and other watchdog groups agree that exposing environmental degradation is increasingly risky for environmental reporters (Sharma 2009). Reporters Without Borders puts it this way:

> In many countries – especially, but not only, those that are not democracies – journalists who specialise in the environment are on the front line of a new war. The violence to which they are subjected concerns us all. It reflects the new issues that have assumed an enormous political and geostrategic importance. (Reporters Without Borders 2009: 1)

There is much at stake in this conflict; wealth, lifestyles, landscapes, species. News media play a vital role in shaping public debate, in reflecting public concerns, in revealing injustices and illegalities, in determining environmental futures. They need the will, the capacity and the support to push for political change and incisive action, now and in coming decades. This is something about which not only news media but those around them should agree.

References

ABC (2003) 'Conservationists "Burnt Off" About Giant Tree Damage', *ABC News Online*, 3 May, www.abc.net.au/news/newsitems/s846182.htm (retrieved August 2008).

Alexander, Jeffrey C. (2006) *The Civil Sphere*. Oxford: Oxford University Press.

Allan, Stuart (2002) *Media, Risk and Science*. Buckingham: Open University Press.

Allan, Stuart (2004) *News Culture*. Maidenhead: Open University Press.

Allan, Stuart (2006) *Online News: Journalism and the Internet*. Maidenhead: Open University Press.

Allan, Stuart, Barbara Adam and Cynthia Carter (eds.) (2000) *Environmental Risks and the Media*. London: Routledge.

Altmann, Carol (2003a) 'Burn-off Kills 350-year-old Tree', *Weekend Australian* (Sydney), 3 May.

Altmann, Carol (2003b) 'War Drums in the Woods', *Australian* (Sydney), 24 July.

Anderson, Alison (1997) *Media, Culture and the Environment*. London: Routledge.

Anderson, Alison and Agnes Marhadour (2007) 'Slick PR? The Media Politics of the Prestige Oil Spill', *Science Communication* 29(1): 96–115.

Associated Press in Berlin (2007) 'Knut the Polar Bear on Cover of Vanity Fair', *Guardian*, 7 April, http://www.guardian.co.uk/media/2007/apr/07/pressand publishing.germany (retrieved April 2010).

Australian (2009) 'The Damage Done by NGOs', *Australian* (Sydney), 18 December.

Barthes, Roland (1977) 'Rhetoric of the Image', pp. 32–51 in R. Barthes, *Image, Music, Text*. London: Fontana.

BBC (2003) 'Giant Tree Devastated by Fire', *BBC News*, 2 June, http://news.bbc.co.uk/2/hi/asia-pacific/2953448.stm (retrieved July 2008).

Beale, Bob (2003) 'Death of a Giant', *Bulletin*, 31 August, http://bulletin.

ninemsn.com.au/bulletin/EdDesk.nsf/printing/971F18555646625ACA256D7
9001E52F1 (retrieved July 2008).

Beck, Ulrich (1992) *Risk Society: Towards a New Modernity*. London: Sage.

Beck, Ulrich (1995) *Ecological Politics in an Age of Risk*. Cambridge: Polity Press.

Beck, Ulrich (1996) 'World Risk Society as Cosmopolitan Society? Ecological Questions in a Framework of Manufactured Uncertainties', *Theory, Culture and Society* 13(4): 1–32.

Beck, Ulrich (1999) *World Risk Society*. Cambridge: Polity Press.

Beck, Ulrich (2000) 'Foreword', pp. xii–xiv in S. Allan, B. Adam and C. Carter (eds.) *Environmental Risks and the Media*. London: Routledge.

Beck, Ulrich (2006) *The Cosmopolitan Vision*. Cambridge: Polity Press.

Beck, Ulrich (2009) *World at Risk*. Cambridge: Polity Press.

Becker, Howard S. (1967) 'Whose Side are We On?' *Social Problems* 14(3): 230–47.

Beder, Sharon (2000) *Global Spin: The Corporate Assault on Environmentalism*. Carlton North: Scribe.

Beder, Sharon (2004) 'Moulding and Manipulating the News', pp. 204–20 in R. White (ed.) *Controversies in Environmental Sociology*. Cambridge: Cambridge University Press.

Bell, Allan (1991) *The Language of News Media*. Oxford: Blackwell.

Bell, Allan (1998) 'The Discourse Structure of News Stories', pp. 64–104 in A. Bell and P. Garrett (eds.) *Approaches to Media Discourse*. Oxford: Blackwell.

Boettger, Conny and Fouad Hamdan (2001) *Greenpeace: Changing the World*. Steinfurt: Edition Rasch & Rohring.

Bonyhady, Tim (2000) *The Colonial Earth*. Carlton South: Melbourne University Press.

Bonyhady, Tim (2003) 'Foreword', p. 5 in G. Edwards (ed.) *Giant: Ancient and Historic Trees*. Geelong: Geelong Gallery.

Bourdieu, Pierre (1991) *Language and Symbolic Power*. Cambridge: Polity Press.

Boykoff, Maxwell and Jules Boykoff (2004) 'Balance as Bias: Global Warming and the US Prestige Press', *Global Environmental Change* 14: 125–36.

Boykoff, Maxwell and Jules Boykoff (2007) 'Climate Change and Journalistic Norms: A Case-study of US Mass-media Coverage', *Geoforum* 38: 1190–204.

Boykoff, Maxwell and Michael Goodman (2009) 'Conspicuous Redemption? Reflections on the Promises and Perils of the "Celebritization" of climate change', *Geoforum* 40(3): 395–406.

Brockington, Dan (2009) *Celebrity and the Environment: Fame, Wealth and Power in Conservation*. London: ZED Books.

Brookes, S. K., A. G. Jordan, R. H. Kimber and J. J. Richardson (1976) 'The Growth of the Environment as a Political Issue in Britain', *British Journal of Political Science* 6(2): 245–55.

Brown, William J. (2010) 'Steve Irwin's Influence on Wildlife Conservation', *Journal of Communication* 60: 73–93.

Carroll, William K. and Robert A. Hackett (2006) 'Democratic Media Activism Through the Lens of Social Movement Theory', *Media, Culture and Society* 28(1): 83–104.

Carson, Rachel (1962) *Silent Spring*. London: Penguin Books.

Carvalho, Anabela (2007) 'Ideological Cultures and Media Discourses on Scientific Knowledge: Rereading News on Climate Change', *Public Understanding of Science* 16: 223–43.

Castells, Manuel (2004) *The Power of Identity*. Malden, MA: Blackwell Publishing.

Castells, Manuel (2007) 'Communication, Power and Counter-power in the Network Society', *International Journal of Communication* 1: 238–66.

Castells, Manuel (2009) *Communication Power*. Oxford: Oxford University Press.

Chapman, Graham, Keval Kumar, Caroline Fraser and Ivor Gaber (1997) *Environmentalism and the Mass Media*. London: Routledge.

Chapman, Jane (2005) *Comparative Media History*. Cambridge: Polity Press.

Chouliaraki, Lilie (2006) *The Spectatorship of Suffering*. London: Sage.

Conboy, Martin (2004) *Journalism: A Critical History*. London: Sage.

Cosgrove, Denis (1994) 'Contested Global Visions: One World, Whole Earth and the Apollo Space Photographs', *Annals of the Association of American Geographers* 84(2): 270–94.

Cottle, Simon (2000) 'TV News, Lay Voices and the Visualisation of Environmental Risks', pp. 29–44 in S. Allan, B. Adam and C. Carter (eds.) *Environmental Risks and the Media*. London: Routledge.

Cottle, Simon (2003) 'News, Public Relations and Power: Mapping the Field', pp. 3–24 in S. Cottle (ed.) *News, Public Relations and Power*. London: Sage.

Cottle, Simon (2006) *Mediatized Conflict*. Maidenhead: Open University Press.

Cottle, Simon (2008) 'Reporting Demonstrations: The Changing Media Politics of Dissent', *Media, Culture and Society* 30(6): 853–72.

Cottle, Simon (2009) *Global Crisis Reporting: Journalism in the Global Age*. Maidenhead: Open University Press.

Cottle, Simon and Mugdha Rai (2006) 'Between Display and Deliberation: Analyzing TV News as Communicative Architecture', *Media, Culture and Society* 28(2): 163–90.

Couldry, Nick (2000) *The Place of Media Power: Pilgrims and Witnesses of the Media Age*. London: Routledge.

Couldry, Nick (2006) *Listening Beyond the Echoes: Media, Ethics, and Agency in an Uncertain World*. Boulder, CO: Paradigm Publishers.

Couldry, Nick, Sonia Livingstone and Tim Markham (2007) *Media Consumption and Public Engagement*. Basingstoke, Hampshire: Palgrave Macmillan.

Couldry, Nick and Tim Markham (2008) 'Troubled Closeness or Satisfied

Distance? Researching Media Consumption and Public Orientation', *Media, Culture and Society* 30(1): 5–21.

Cox, Robert (2010) *Environmental Communication and the Public Sphere.* Thousand Oaks, CA: Sage.

Craig, Geoffrey (2002) 'The Spectacle of the Street: An Analysis of Media Coverage of Protests at the 2000 Melbourne World Economic Forum', *Australian Journal of Communication* 29(1): 39–52.

Curran, James (1991) 'Rethinking the Media as a Public Sphere', pp. 27–57 in P. Dahlgren and C. Sparks (eds.) *Communication and Citizenship: Journalism and the Public Sphere in the New Media Age.* London: Routledge.

Curran, James (2002) *Media and Power.* London: Routledge.

Dahlgren, Peter (1991) 'Introduction', pp. 1–24 in P. Dahlgren and C. Sparks (eds.) *Communication and Citizenship: Journalism and the Public Sphere in the New Media Age.* London: Routledge.

Dahlgren, Peter (2009) *Media and Political Engagement: Citizens, Communication, and Democracy.* New York: Cambridge University Press.

Darby, Andrew (2003) 'Fury as Nation's Biggest Tree Goes up in Flames', *Sydney Morning Herald* (Sydney), 1 May.

Darby, Andrew with AAP (2003) 'Giant Tree Damaged During Burn-off', *Age* (Melbourne), 1 May.

Davies, Nick (2008) *Flat Earth News: An Award-winning Reporter Exposes Falsehood, Distortion and Propaganda in the Global Media.* London: Chatto & Windus.

Davis, Aeron (2003) 'Public Relations and News Sources', pp. 27–42 in S. Cottle (ed.) *News, Public Relations and Power.* London: Sage.

Davis, Aeron (2009) 'Journalist-Source Relations, Mediated Reflexivity and the Politics of Politics', *Journalism Studies* 10(2): 204–19.

Dawson, Bill (2009–10) 'The Beat: Top Universities Rethink How to Prepare E-beat Journalists', *SEJ Journal* 19(4): 20–2.

Deacon, David, Michael Pickering, Peter Golding and Graham Murdock (2007) *Researching Communications: A Practical Guide to Methods in Media and Cultural Analysis.* London: Arnold.

DeLuca, Kevin Michael (1999) *Image Politics.* New York: Guilford Press.

DeLuca, Kevin Michael and Anne Teresa Demo (2000) 'Imaging Nature: Watkins, Yosemite, and the Birth of Environmentalism', *Critical Studies in Media Communication* 17(3): 241–60.

DeLuca, Kevin Michael and Jennifer Peeples (2002) 'From Public Sphere to Public Screen: Democracy, Activism, and the "Violence" of Seattle', *Critical Studies in Media Communication* 19(2): 125–51.

Downey, John (2007) 'Participation and/or Deliberation? The Internet as Tool for Achieving Radical Democratic Aims', pp. 108–29 in L. Dahlberg and E. Siapera (eds.) *Radical Democracy and the Internet: Interrogating Theory and Practice.* Basingstoke: Palgrave Macmillan.

Downs, Anthony (1972) 'Up and Down with Ecology: the "Issue-Attention" Cycle', *The Public Interest* 28: 38–50.

Doyle, Julie (2007) 'Picturing the Clima(c)tic: Greenpeace and the Representational Politics of Climate Change Communication', *Science as Culture* 16(2): 129–50.

Doyle, Julie (2009) 'Climate Action and Environmental Activism: The Role of Environmental NGOs and Grassroots Movements in the Global Politics of Climate Change', pp. 103–16 in T. Boyce and J. Lewis (eds.) *Climate Change and the Media*. New York: Peter Lang.

Dvorak, Phred (2009) 'The Hunt for a Clear Picture of Polar Bears' Future', *Wall Street Journal*, 31 December, http://online.wsj.com/article/SB126221385046310927.html (retrieved January 2010).

Dykstra, Peter (2008) 'Magic Number: A Sketchy "Fact" about Polar Bears keeps going . . . and going . . . and going', *SEJ Journal* 18(2): 5–7.

Edwards, Geoffrey (2003) *Giant: Ancient and Historic Trees*. Geelong: Geelong Gallery.

Edwards, Michael (2009) *Civil Society*. Cambridge: Polity Press.

Entman, Robert M. (1993) 'Framing: Toward Clarification of a Fractured Paradigm', *Journal of Communication* 43(4): 51–8.

Ericson, Richard V., Patricia M. Baranek and Janet B.L. Chan (1989) *Negotiating Control: A Study of News Sources*. Milton Keynes: Open University Press.

Fahn, James (2009) 'Climate Change: How to Report the Story of the Century', http://www.scidev.net/en/science-communication/science-journalism/practical-guides/ (retrieved August 2009).

Fairclough, Norman (1998) 'Political Discourse in the Media: An Analytical Framework', pp. 142–62 in A. Bell and P. Garrett (eds.) *Approaches to Media Discourse*. Oxford: Blackwell.

Featherstone, Mike (1993) 'Global and Local Cultures', pp. 169–87 in J. Bird, B. Curtis, T. Putnam, G. Robertson and L. Tickner (eds.) *Mapping the Futures: Local Cultures, Global Change*. London: Routledge.

Flew, Terry (2008) *New Media: An Introduction*. South Melbourne: Oxford University Press.

Forestry Tasmania (2003a) 'Florentine Giant Stands Tall', media release, 15 April.

Forestry Tasmania (2003b) 'Giant Trees Keep Names', media release, 15 December.

Forestry Tasmania (2005a) 'Tasmania's Ten Tallest Trees', http://www.giant-trees.com.au/tall.htm (retrieved August 2006).

Forestry Tasmania (2005b) 'Tasmania's Ten Most Massive Trees', http://www.gianttrees.com.au/massive.htm (retrieved August 2006).

Fowler, Roger (1991) *Language in the News: Discourse and Ideology in the Press*. London: Routledge.

Franklin, Bob, Martin Hamer, Mark Hanna, Marie Kinsey and John E. Richardson (2005) *Key Concepts in Journalism Studies*. London: Sage.

Franklin, Sarah, Celia Lury and Jackie Stacey (2000) *Global Nature, Global Culture*. London: Sage.

Fraser, Nancy (1992) 'Rethinking the Public Sphere: A Contribution to the Critique of Actually Existing Democracy', pp. 109–42 in C. Calhoun (ed.) *Habermas and the Public Sphere*. Cambridge, MA: The MIT Press.

Furedi, Frank (2009) 'Much Ado About Nothing in Denmark', *Australian* (Sydney), 21 December.

Galtung, Johan and Mari Holmboe Ruge (1965) 'The Structure of Foreign News', *Journal of International Peace Research* 1: 64–90.

Gamson, Joshua (1994) *Claims to Fame: Celebrity in Contemporary America*. Berkeley, CA: University of California Press.

Gans, Herbert J. (1979) *Deciding What's News*. New York: Pantheon Books.

Garcia, David and Geert Lovink (1997) 'The ABC of Tactical Media', http://www.nettime.org/Lists-Archives/nettime-l-9705/msg00096.html (retrieved November 2005).

Garrett, Peter and Allan Bell (1998) 'Media and Discourse: A Critical Overview', pp. 1–20 in A. Bell and P. Garrett (eds.) *Approaches to Media Discourse*. Oxford: Blackwell.

Giddens, Anthony (2009) *The Politics of Climate Change*. Cambridge: Polity Press.

Gitlin, Todd (1980) *The Whole World Is Watching*. Berkeley, CA: University of California Press.

Goldenberg, Suzanne (2009) 'Obama's Key Climate Bill hit by $45 m PR Campaign', *Guardian* (Manchester), 13 May.

Goode, Erich and Nachman Ben-Yehuda (1994) *Moral Panics: The Social Construction of Deviance*. Oxford: Blackwell.

Griffiths, Tom (1990) 'History and Natural History: Conservation Movements in Conflict?', pp. 87–109 in D. J. Mulvaney (ed.) *The Humanities and the Australian Environment*. Canberra: Australian Academy of the Humanities.

Guardian (2009) 'Fourteen Days to Seal History's Judgment on this Generation', *Guardian*, 7 December, http://www.guardian.co.uk/commentisfree/2009/dec/06/copenhagen-editorial (retrieved December 2009).

Guggenheim, Davis (2006) *An Inconvenient Truth*. Paramount Classics, USA.

Habermas, Jurgen (1962/1989) *The Structural Transformation of the Public Sphere: An Inquiry into a Category of Bourgeois Society*. Cambridge: Polity Press.

Hall, Stuart, Chas Critcher, Tony Jefferson, John Clarke and Brian Roberts (1978) *Policing the Crisis: Mugging, the State, and Law and Order*. New York: Holmes & Meier.

Hallin, Daniel C. (1986) *The 'Uncensored War': The Media and Vietnam*. New York: Oxford University Press.

References

Hallin, Daniel C. and Paolo Mancini (2004) *Comparing Media Systems: Three Models of Media and Politics*. Cambridge: Cambridge University Press.

Halloran, James D., Philip Elliott and Graham Murdock (1970) *Demonstrations and Communication: a Case Study*. Harmondsworth: Penguin Books.

Hannigan, John A. (2006) *Environmental Sociology*. London: Routledge.

Hansen, Anders (1993) 'Greenpeace and Press Coverage of Environmental Issues', pp. 150–78 in A. Hansen (ed.) *The Mass Media and Environmental Issues*. Leicester: Leicester University Press.

Hansen, Anders (2000) 'Claims-making and Framing in British Newspaper Coverage of the "Brent Spar" Controversy', pp. 55–72 in S. Allan, B. Adam and C. Carter (eds.) *Environmental Risk and the Media*. London: Routledge.

Hansen, Anders, Simon Cottle, Ralph Negrine and Chris Newbold (1998) *Mass Communication Research Methods*. Basingstoke: Palgrave.

Hansen, Anders and David Machin (2008) 'Visually Branding the Environment: Climate Change as a Marketing Opportunity', *Discourse Studies* 10(6): 777–94.

Hay, Peter (1991) 'Destabilising Tasmanian Politics: The Key Role of the Greens', *Bulletin of the Centre for Tasmanian Historical Studies* 3(2): 60–70.

Hay, Peter (2002) *Main Currents in Western Environmental Thought*. Sydney: UNSW Press.

Head, Lesley (2000) *Cultural Landscapes and Environmental Change*. London: Arnold.

Herman, Edward and Noam Chomsky (1988) *Manufacturing Consent: The Political Economy of the Mass Media*. New York: Pantheon.

Hilgartner, Stephen and Charles L. Bosk (1988) 'The Rise and Fall of Social Problems: A Public Arenas Model', *American Journal of Sociology* 94(1): 53–78.

Hutchins, Brett and Libby Lester (2006) 'Environmental Protest and Tap-dancing with the Media in the Information Age', *Media, Culture and Society* 28(3): 433–51.

Hutchins, Brett and Libby Lester (forthcoming 2010) 'Politics, Power and Online Protest in an Age of Environmental Conflict', in S. Cottle and L. Lester (eds.) *Transnational Protests and the Media*. New York: Peter Lang.

Joppke, Christian (1991) 'Social Movements During Cycles of Issue Attention: the Decline of the Anti-Nuclear Energy Movements in West Germany and the USA', *British Journal of Sociology* 42(1): 43–60.

Kirkpatrick, J.B. (1998) 'The Politics of the Media and Ecological Ethics', pp. 36–41 in R. Wills and R. Hobbs (eds.) *Ecology for Everyone: Communicating Ecology to Scientists, the Public and the Politicians*. Chipping North: Surrey Beatty and Sons.

Knightley, Phillip (2000) *The First Casualty: The War Correspondent as Hero and Myth-maker from the Crimea to Kosovo*. London: Prion Books.

Krauss, Clifford (2006) 'Debate on Global Warming has Polar Bear Hunting in its Sights', *New York Times*, 27 May, http://query.nytimes.com/gst/fullpage. html?res=9B0CE3D91E3EF934A15756C0A9609C8B63 (retrieved May 2009).

Kudo, Mitsuru (2008) 'A Comparative Analysis of the Press Coverage of the Whaling Conflict in Australia and Japan in 2005–2006', unpublished MA thesis, Journalism, Media and Communications, University of Tasmania, Hobart.

Leigh, David and Afua Hirsch (2009) 'How Trafigura tried to Limit the Damage through Spin', *Guardian* (Manchester), 14 May.

Lester, Libby (2006a) 'We Too are Green: Public Relations, Symbolic Power and the Tasmanian Wilderness Conflict', *Media International Australia incorporating Culture and Policy* 121: 52–64.

Lester, Libby (2006b) 'Journalism, Reflexivity and the Natural State', *Australian Journal of Communication* 33(2, 3): 75–88.

Lester, Libby (2007) *Giving Ground: Media and Environmental Conflict in Tasmania*. Hobart: Quintus.

Lester, Libby (2010a) 'Journalism and Celebrity Politics', pp. 141–58 in V. Rupar (ed.) *Journalism and Meaning-making: Reading the Newspaper*. Cresskill, NJ: Hampton Press.

Lester, Libby (forthcoming 2010b) 'Big Tree, Small News: Media Access, Symbolic Power and Strategic Access', *Journalism: Theory, Practice and Criticism*, 11(4).

Lester, Libby and Simon Cottle (2009) 'Visualizing Climate Change: Television News and Ecological Citizenship', *International Journal of Communications* 3: 920–36.

Lester, Libby and Brett Hutchins (2009) 'Power Games: Environmental Protest, News Media and the Internet', *Media, Culture and Society* 31(4): 579–96.

Lewis, Justin, Andrew Williams, Bob Franklin, James Thomas and Nick Mosdell (2008) 'The Quality and Independence of British Journalism: Tracking the Changes over 20 Years'. Journalism and Public Trust Project and Cardiff University.

Lindahl Elliot, Nils (2006) *Mediating Nature*. Abingdon: Routledge.

Lohrey, Amanda (2002) 'Groundswell: The Rise of the Greens', *Quarterly Essay* 8: 1–86.

Lomborg, Bjorn (2007) *Cool It: The Skeptical Environmentalist's Guide to Global Warming*. New York: Alfred A. Knopf.

Lovink, Geert (2002) *Dark Fiber: Tracking Critical Internet Culture*. Cambridge, MA: MIT Press.

Lowe, Philip and Jane Goyder (1983) *Environmental Groups in Politics*. London: George Allen & Unwin.

Lowe, Philip and David Morrison (1984) 'Bad News or Good News: Environmental Politics and the Mass Media', *Sociological Review* 32: 75–90.

McGaurr, Lyn and Libby Lester (2009) 'Complementary Problems, Competing

Risks: Climate Change, Nuclear Energy, and the Australian', pp. 174–85 in T. Boyce and J. Lewis (eds.) *Climate Change and the Media*. New York: Peter Lang.

McGreal, Chris (2009) 'Canadian Governor asks for Tasty Treat – Raw Seal Heart', *Guardian* (Manchester), 26 May.

Macnaghten, Phil and John Urry (1998) *Contested Natures*. London: Sage.

McNair, Brian (2006) *Cultural Chaos: Journalism, News and Power in a Globalised World*. London: Routledge.

Manning, Paul (2001) *News and News Sources: A Critical Introduction*. London: Sage.

Marshall, P. David (2005) 'Intimately Intertwined in the Most Public Way: Celebrity and Journalism', pp. 19–29 in S. Allan (ed.) *Journalism: Critical Issues*. Maidenhead: Open University Press.

Mayerfeld Bell, Michael (1998) *Invitation to Environmental Sociology*. Thousand Oaks, CA: Sage.

Mazur, Allan (1990) 'Nuclear Power, Chemical Hazards, and the Quantity of Reporting', *Minerva* 28(3): 294–323.

Mercury (2002) 'Foes Measure Up for Giant', *Mercury* (Hobart), 26 June.

Mercury (2003) 'Tasmania's Top Tree Survives the Flames', *Mercury* (Hobart), 16 April.

Meyer, David S. and Joshua Gamson (1995) 'The Challenge of Cultural Elites: Celebrities and Social Movements', *Sociological Inquiry* 65(2): 181–206.

Miller, M. Mark and Bonnie Parnell Riechert (2000) 'Interest Group Strategies and Journalistic Norms: News Media Framing of Environmental Issues', pp. 45–54 in S. Allan, B. Adam, and C. Carter (eds.) *Environmental Risks and the Media*. London: Routledge.

Molotch, Harvey (1979) 'Media and Movements', pp. 71–92 in M.N. Zald and J.D. McCarthy (eds.) *The Dynamics of Social Movements: Resource Mobilisation, Social Control, and Tactics*. Cambridge, MA: Winthrop.

Molotch, Harvey and Marilyn Lester (1975) 'Accidental News: The Great Oil Spill as Local Occurrence and National Event', *American Journal of Sociology* 81(2): 235–60.

Monbiot, George (2002) 'An Activist's Guide to Exploiting the Media', http://www.urban75/Action/media.html (retrieved February 2002).

Monbiot, George (2006) *Heat: How to Stop the Planet Burning*. London: Penguin Books.

Monbiot, George (2008) *Bring on the Apocalypse: Six Arguments for Global Justice*. London: Atlantic Books.

Murdock, Graham (1981) 'Political Deviance: The Press Presentation of a Militant Mass Demonstration', pp. 206–25 in S. Cohen and J. Young (eds.) *The Manufacture of News: Social Problems, Deviance and the Mass Media*. London: Constable.

Nagtzaam, Gerry and Pete Lentini (2008) 'Vigilantes on the High Seas? The

Sea Shepherds and Political Violence', *Terrorism and Political Violence* 20: 110–33.

Nash, Roderick Frazier (2001) *Wilderness and the American Mind*. New Haven, CT: Yale Nota Bene.

Neuzil, Mark (2008) *The Environment and the Press: From Adventure Writing to Advocacy*. Evanston, IL: Northwestern University Press.

Neuzil, Mark and William Kovarik (1996) *Mass Media and Environmental Conflict*. Thousand Oaks, CA: Sage.

Olesen, Thomas (2008) 'Activist Journalism?', *Journalism Practice* 2(2): 245–63.

O'Neill, Saffron and Sophie Nicholson-Cole (2009) '"Fear Won't Do It": Promoting Positive Engagement with Climate Change Through Visual and Iconic Representations', *Science Communication* 30(3): 355–79.

Paine, Michelle (2003a) 'Doubt Cast on Scorched Tree', *Mercury* (Hobart), 1 May.

Paine, Michelle (2003b) 'Giant Tree "Cooked to Death"', *Mercury* (Hobart), 3 May.

Parks and Wildlife Service, Tasmania (1999) *Tasmanian Wilderness World Heritage Area Management Plan*. Hobart: Parks and Wildlife Service.

Parlour, J.W. and S. Schatzow (1978) 'The Mass Media and Public Concern for Environmental Problems in Canada, 1960–1972', *International Journal of Environmental Studies* 13(1): 9–17.

PETA (2009) 'PETA's History: Compassion in Action', http://www.peta.org/factsheet/files/FactsheetDisplay.asp?ID=107 (retrieved June 2009).

Pew Project for Excellence in Journalism (2009) *The State of the News Media*, http://www.stateofthemedia.org/2009/index.htm (retrieved April 2010).

Pew Research Centre for the People and the Press (2010) 'Economy, Jobs Trump All Other Policy Priorities in 2009', http://people-press.org/report/485/economy-top-policy-priority (retrieved April 2010).

Pollack, Henry N. (2005) *Uncertain Science . . . Uncertain World*. Cambridge: Cambridge University Press.

Pritchard, Paul and Mark Townsend (2003) 'World's Tallest Tree is Cooked Alive', *Guardian*, 1 June, http://www.guardian.co.uk/world/2003/jun/01/australia.theobserver1 (retrieved August 2008).

Ramson, William (1990) 'Wasteland to Wilderness: Changing Perceptions of the Environment', pp. 5–19 in D.J. Mulvaney (ed.) *The Humanities and the Australian Environment*. Canberra: Australian Academy of the Humanities.

Reporters Without Borders (2009) 'The Dangers for Journalists Who Expose Environmental Issues', http://www.rsf.org/IMG/rapport_en_md.pdf (retrieved December 2009).

Robertson, Alexa (2010) *Mediated Cosmopolitanism*. Cambridge: Polity Press.

Rose, Danny (2003) 'Giant Trees Lose Names', *Mercury* (Hobart), 15 December.

Rose, Gillian (2001) *Visual Methodologies: An Introduction to the Interpretation of Visual Materials*. London: Sage.

References

Royal Society of Chemistry (2007) 'Myth of Cooling Towers is Symptomatic of Global Warming Information Shortage', http://www.rsc.org/AboutUs/News/PressReleases/2007/coolingtowersmyth.asp (retrieved September 2008).

Rucht, Dieter (2004) 'The Quadruple "A": Media Strategies of Protest Movements since the 1960s', pp. 29–58 in W. van de Donk, B.D. Loader, P.G. Nixon and D. Rucht (eds.) *Cyberprotest: New Media, Citzens and Social Movements*. London: Routledge.

Ryan, Noel (2003) 'Wasteland', *Illawarra Mercury* (Wollongong), 8 July.

Schama, Simon (1995) *Landscape and Memory*. New York: Alfred A. Knopf.

Schlesinger, Philip (1990) 'Rethinking the Sociology of Journalism: Source Strategies and the Limits of Media-Centrism', pp. 61–83 in M. Ferguson (ed.) *Public Communication: the New Imperatives*. London: Sage.

Schlesinger, Philip (2006) 'Is there a Crisis in British Journalism?', *Media, Culture and Society* 28(2): 299–307.

Schlesinger, Philip and Howard Tumber (1994) *Reporting Crime*. Oxford: Clarendon Press.

Schoenfeld, A. Clay, Robert F. Meier and Robert J. Griffin (1979) 'Constructing a Social Problem: the Press and the Environment', *Social Problems* 27(1): 38–61.

Schudson, Michael (2003) *The Sociology of News*. New York: W. W. Norton & Company.

Sharma, Betwa (2009) 'Threats to Environmental Journalists on the Rise', *Columbia Journalism Review*, 15 December, http://www.cjr.org/the_observatory/threats_to_environmental_journ.php (retrieved December 2009).

Sheail, John (2002) *An Environmental History of Twentieth-Century Britian*. Basingstoke: Palgrave.

Smith, Joe (2005) 'Dangerous News: Media Decision Making about Climate Change Risk', *Risk Analysis* 25(6): 1471–82.

Solesbury, William (1976) 'The Environmental Agenda: An Illustration of How Situations May Become Political Issues and Issues May Demand Responses from Government: or How They May Not', *Public Administration* 54: 379–97.

Stedman, Michael (2010) 'Whale Defenders Vow to Press on', *Mercury* (Hobart), 8 February.

Stevenson, Nick (2002) *Understanding Media Cultures: Social Theory and Mass Communication*. London: Sage.

Szerszynski, Bronislaw (2006) 'Local Landscapes and Global Belonging: Toward a Situated Citizenship of the Environment', pp. 75–100 in A. Dobson and D. Bell (eds.) *Environmental Citizenship*. Cambridge, MA: MIT Press.

Szerszynski, Bronislaw and Mark Toogood (2000) 'Global Citizenship, the Environment and the Media', pp. 201–17 in S. Allan, B. Adam and C. Carter (eds.) *Environmental Risks and the Media*. London: Routledge.

Szerszynski, Bronislaw and John Urry (2002) 'Cultures of Cosmopolitanism', *The Sociological Review* 50(4): 461–81.

Szerszynski, Bronislaw and John Urry (2006) 'Visuality, Mobility and the Cosmopolitan: Inhabiting the World from Afar', *The British Journal of Sociology* 57(1): 113–31.

Szerszynski, Bronislaw, John Urry and Greg Myers (2000) 'Mediating Global Citizenship', pp. 97–114 in J. Smith (ed.) *The Daily Globe: Environmental Change, the Public and the Media*. London: Earthscan.

Thompson, John B. (1995) *The Media and Modernity: A Social Theory of the Media*. Cambridge: Polity Press.

Thompson, John B. (2005) 'The New Visibility', *Theory, Culture and Society* 22(6): 31–51.

Thrall, A. Trevor, Jaime Lollio-Fakhreddine, Jon Berent, Lana Donnelly, Wes Herrin, Zachary Paquette, Rebecca Wenglinski and Amy Wyatt (2008) 'Star Power: Celebrity Advocacy and the Evolution of the Public Sphere', *The International Journal of Press/Politics* 13(4): 362–85.

Torrance, Robert M. (1998) *Encompassing Nature: A Sourcebook*. Washington DC: Counterpoint.

Tranter, Bruce (2004) 'The Environment Movement: Where to from Here?', pp. 185–203 in R. White (ed.) *Controversies in Environmental Sociology*. Cambridge: Cambridge University Press.

Tuchman, Gaye (1972) 'Objectivity as Strategic Ritual,' *American Journal of Sociology* 77: 660–79.

Tuchman, Gaye (1978) *Making News: A Study in the Construction of Reality*. New York: Free Press.

Turner, Graeme (2004) *Understanding Celebrity*. London: Sage.

Turner, Graeme, Frances Bonner and P. David Marshall (2000) *Fame Games: The Production of Celebrity in Australia*. Cambridge: Cambridge University Press.

Ungar, Sheldon (1998) 'Bringing the Issue Back In: Comparing the Marketability of the Ozone Hole and Global Warming', *Social Problems* 45(4): 510–27.

Urry, John (1999) 'Globalization and Citizenship', *Journal of World-Systems Research* 2: 311–24.

Urry, John (2000) 'The Global Media and Cosmopolitanism', http://www.lancs.ac.uk/fass/sociology/papers/urry-global-media.pdf (retrieved August 2008).

Urry, John (2002) *The Tourist Gaze*. London: Sage.

van Dijk, Teun (1991) 'The Interdisciplinary Study of News as Discourse', pp. 108–20 in K.B. Jensen and N.W. Jankowski (eds.) *A Handbook of Qualitative Methodologies for Mass Communication Research*. London: Routledge.

Waddington, David (1992) *Contemporary Issues in Public Disorder*. London: Routledge.

Waisbord, Silvio and Enrique Peruzzotti (2009) 'The Environmental Story that Wasn't: Advocacy, Journalism and the Asambleismo Movement in Argentina', *Media, Culture and Society* 31(5): 691–709.

Weekend Australian (2009) 'Hacked Climate Emails "Ignored"', *Weekend Australian* (Sydney), 5–6 December.

Weyler, Rex (2004) *Greenpeace: An Insider's Account*. London: Rodale.

Whelan, Kathleen (1993) *Photography of The Age*. Sydney: Hale and Iremonger.

Wilderness Society (2003) 'Forestry Tasmania Admits Killing Australia's Largest Known Living Thing', media release, 9 December.

Wilkinson, Marian (2009) 'Scientists Hit Back at Climate Scepticism', *Sydney Morning Herald*, 1 August, http://www.smh.com.au/environment/global-warming/scientists-hit-back-at-climate-scepticism-20090731-e4fd.html (retrieved August 2009).

Wilson, Alexander (1992) *The Culture of Nature: North American Landscape from Disney to the Exxon Valdez*. Cambridge, MA: Blackwell.

Wolfsfeld, Gadi (1997) *Media and Political Conflict: News from the Middle East*. Cambridge: Cambridge University Press.

Zelizer, Barbie (2004) *Taking Journalism Seriously: News and the Academy*. Thousand Oaks, CA: Sage.

Index

Index